SCRIPTURE
JOURNAL

ENGLISH STANDARD VERSION

1–2 SAMUEL

CROSSWAY

WHEATON, ILLINOIS — ESV.ORG

PREFACE

The Bible

The words of the Bible are the very words of God our Creator speaking to us. They are completely truthful;[1] they are pure;[2] they are powerful;[3] and they are wise and righteous.[4] We should read these words with reverence and awe,[5] and with joy and delight.[6] Through these words God gives us eternal life,[7] and daily nourishes our spiritual lives.[8]

The ESV Translation

The English Standard Version® (ESV®) stands in the classic stream of English Bible translations that goes back nearly five centuries. In this stream, accurate faithfulness to the original text is combined with simplicity, beauty, and dignity of expression. Our goal has been to carry forward this legacy for this generation and generations to come.

The ESV is an "essentially literal" translation that seeks as far as possible to reproduce the meaning and structure of the original text and the personal style of each Bible writer. We have sought to be "as literal as possible" while maintaining clear expression and literary excellence. Therefore the ESV is well suited for both personal reading and church ministry, for devotional reflection and serious study, and for Scripture memorization.

---

[1] Ps. 119:160; Prov. 30:5; Titus 1:2; Heb. 6:18 [2] Ps. 12:6 [3] Jer. 23:29; Heb. 4:12; 1 Pet. 1:23
[4] Ps. 19:7–11 [5] Deut. 28:58; Ps. 119:74; Isa. 66:2 [6] Ps. 19:7–11; 119:14, 97, 103; Jer. 15:16
[7] John 6:68; 1 Pet. 1:23 [8] Deut. 32:46; Matt. 4:4

The ESV Publishing Team

The ESV publishing team has included more than a hundred people. The fourteen-member Translation Oversight Committee benefited from the work of fifty biblical experts serving as Translation Review Scholars and from the comments of the more than fifty members of the Advisory Council. This international team from many denominations shares a common commitment to the truth of God's Word and to historic Christian orthodoxy.

To God's Honor and Praise

We know that no Bible translation is perfect; but we also know that God uses imperfect and inadequate things to his honor and praise. So to God the Father, Son, and Holy Spirit—and to his people—we offer what we have done, with our prayers that it may prove useful, with gratitude for much help given, and with ongoing wonder that our God should ever have entrusted to us so momentous a task.

To God alone be the glory!
The Translation Oversight Committee

1 SAMUEL

The Birth of Samuel

1 There was a certain man of Ramathaim-zophim of the hill country of Ephraim whose name was Elkanah the son of Jeroham, son of Elihu, son of Tohu, son of Zuph, an Ephrathite. ²He had two wives. The name of the one was Hannah, and the name of the other, Peninnah. And Peninnah had children, but Hannah had no children.

³Now this man used to go up year by year from his city to worship and to sacrifice to the LORD of hosts at Shiloh, where the two sons of Eli, Hophni and Phinehas, were priests of the LORD. ⁴On the day when Elkanah sacrificed, he would give portions to Peninnah his wife and to all her sons and daughters. ⁵But to Hannah he gave a double portion, because he loved her, though the LORD had closed her womb. ⁶And her rival used to provoke her grievously to irritate her, because the LORD had closed her womb. ⁷So it went on year by year. As often as she went up to the house of the LORD, she used to provoke her. Therefore Hannah wept and would not eat. ⁸And Elkanah, her husband, said to her, "Hannah, why do you weep? And why do you not eat? And why is your heart sad? Am I not more to you than ten sons?"

⁹After they had eaten and drunk in Shiloh, Hannah rose. Now Eli the priest was sitting on the seat beside the doorpost of the temple of the LORD. ¹⁰She was deeply distressed and prayed

to the LORD and wept bitterly. ¹¹ And she vowed a vow and said, "O LORD of hosts, if you will indeed look on the affliction of your servant and remember me and not forget your servant, but will give to your servant a son, then I will give him to the LORD all the days of his life, and no razor shall touch his head."

¹² As she continued praying before the LORD, Eli observed her mouth. ¹³ Hannah was speaking in her heart; only her lips moved, and her voice was not heard. Therefore Eli took her to be a drunken woman. ¹⁴ And Eli said to her, "How long will you go on being drunk? Put your wine away from you." ¹⁵ But Hannah answered, "No, my lord, I am a woman troubled in spirit. I have drunk neither wine nor strong drink, but I have been pouring out my soul before the LORD. ¹⁶ Do not regard your servant as a worthless woman, for all along I have been speaking out of my great anxiety and vexation." ¹⁷ Then Eli answered, "Go in peace, and the God of Israel grant your petition that you have made to him." ¹⁸ And she said, "Let your servant find favor in your eyes." Then the woman went her way and ate, and her face was no longer sad.

¹⁹ They rose early in the morning and worshiped before the LORD; then they went back to their house at Ramah. And Elkanah knew Hannah his wife, and the LORD remembered her. ²⁰ And in due time Hannah conceived and bore a son, and she called his name Samuel, for she said, "I have asked for him from the LORD."

Samuel Given to the LORD

²¹ The man Elkanah and all his house went up to offer to the LORD the yearly sacrifice and to pay his vow. ²² But Hannah did not go up, for she said to her husband, "As soon as the

child is weaned, I will bring him, so that he may appear in the presence of the LORD and dwell there forever." ²³ Elkanah her husband said to her, "Do what seems best to you; wait until you have weaned him; only, may the LORD establish his word." So the woman remained and nursed her son until she weaned him. ²⁴ And when she had weaned him, she took him up with her, along with a three-year-old bull, an ephah of flour, and a skin of wine, and she brought him to the house of the LORD at Shiloh. And the child was young. ²⁵ Then they slaughtered the bull, and they brought the child to Eli. ²⁶ And she said, "Oh, my lord! As you live, my lord, I am the woman who was standing here in your presence, praying to the LORD. ²⁷ For this child I prayed, and the LORD has granted me my petition that I made to him. ²⁸ Therefore I have lent him to the LORD. As long as he lives, he is lent to the LORD."

And he worshiped the LORD there.

Hannah's Prayer

2 And Hannah prayed and said,

> "My heart exults in the LORD;
>> my horn is exalted in the LORD.
> My mouth derides my enemies,
>> because I rejoice in your salvation.

²
> "There is none holy like the LORD:
>> for there is none besides you;
>> there is no rock like our God.

³
> Talk no more so very proudly,
>> let not arrogance come from your mouth;

for the LORD is a God of knowledge,
    and by him actions are weighed.
4 The bows of the mighty are broken,
    but the feeble bind on strength.
5 Those who were full have hired themselves out for
    bread,
    but those who were hungry have ceased to
      hunger.
The barren has borne seven,
    but she who has many children is forlorn.
6 The LORD kills and brings to life;
    he brings down to Sheol and raises up.
7 The LORD makes poor and makes rich;
    he brings low and he exalts.
8 He raises up the poor from the dust;
    he lifts the needy from the ash heap
to make them sit with princes
    and inherit a seat of honor.
For the pillars of the earth are the LORD's,
    and on them he has set the world.

9 "He will guard the feet of his faithful ones,
    but the wicked shall be cut off in darkness,
    for not by might shall a man prevail.
10 The adversaries of the LORD shall be broken to
    pieces;
    against them he will thunder in heaven.
The LORD will judge the ends of the earth;
    he will give strength to his king
    and exalt the horn of his anointed."

¹¹ Then Elkanah went home to Ramah. And the boy was ministering to the Lord in the presence of Eli the priest.

Eli's Worthless Sons

¹² Now the sons of Eli were worthless men. They did not know the Lord. ¹³ The custom of the priests with the people was that when any man offered sacrifice, the priest's servant would come, while the meat was boiling, with a three-pronged fork in his hand, ¹⁴ and he would thrust it into the pan or kettle or cauldron or pot. All that the fork brought up the priest would take for himself. This is what they did at Shiloh to all the Israelites who came there. ¹⁵ Moreover, before the fat was burned, the priest's servant would come and say to the man who was sacrificing, "Give meat for the priest to roast, for he will not accept boiled meat from you but only raw." ¹⁶ And if the man said to him, "Let them burn the fat first, and then take as much as you wish," he would say, "No, you must give it now, and if not, I will take it by force." ¹⁷ Thus the sin of the young men was very great in the sight of the Lord, for the men treated the offering of the Lord with contempt.

¹⁸ Samuel was ministering before the Lord, a boy clothed with a linen ephod. ¹⁹ And his mother used to make for him a little robe and take it to him each year when she went up with her husband to offer the yearly sacrifice. ²⁰ Then Eli would bless Elkanah and his wife, and say, "May the Lord give you children by this woman for the petition she asked of the Lord." So then they would return to their home.

²¹ Indeed the Lord visited Hannah, and she conceived and bore three sons and two daughters. And the boy Samuel grew in the presence of the Lord.

Eli Rebukes His Sons

²² Now Eli was very old, and he kept hearing all that his sons were doing to all Israel, and how they lay with the women who were serving at the entrance to the tent of meeting. ²³ And he said to them, "Why do you do such things? For I hear of your evil dealings from all these people. ²⁴ No, my sons; it is no good report that I hear the people of the LORD spreading abroad. ²⁵ If someone sins against a man, God will mediate for him, but if someone sins against the LORD, who can intercede for him?" But they would not listen to the voice of their father, for it was the will of the LORD to put them to death.

²⁶ Now the boy Samuel continued to grow both in stature and in favor with the LORD and also with man.

The LORD Rejects Eli's Household

²⁷ And there came a man of God to Eli and said to him, "Thus says the LORD, 'Did I indeed reveal myself to the house of your father when they were in Egypt subject to the house of Pharaoh? ²⁸ Did I choose him out of all the tribes of Israel to be my priest, to go up to my altar, to burn incense, to wear an ephod before me? I gave to the house of your father all my offerings by fire from the people of Israel. ²⁹ Why then do you scorn my sacrifices and my offerings that I commanded for my dwelling, and honor your sons above me by fattening yourselves on the choicest parts of every offering of my people Israel?' ³⁰ Therefore the LORD, the God of Israel, declares: 'I promised that your house and the house of your father should go in and out before me forever,' but now the LORD declares: 'Far be it from me, for those who honor me I will honor, and those who despise me shall be lightly esteemed. ³¹ Behold, the days are coming when I will

cut off your strength and the strength of your father's house, so that there will not be an old man in your house. ³²Then in distress you will look with envious eye on all the prosperity that shall be bestowed on Israel, and there shall not be an old man in your house forever. ³³The only one of you whom I shall not cut off from my altar shall be spared to weep his eyes out to grieve his heart, and all the descendants of your house shall die by the sword of men. ³⁴And this that shall come upon your two sons, Hophni and Phinehas, shall be the sign to you: both of them shall die on the same day. ³⁵And I will raise up for myself a faithful priest, who shall do according to what is in my heart and in my mind. And I will build him a sure house, and he shall go in and out before my anointed forever. ³⁶And everyone who is left in your house shall come to implore him for a piece of silver or a loaf of bread and shall say, "Please put me in one of the priests' places, that I may eat a morsel of bread."'"

The LORD Calls Samuel

3 Now the boy Samuel was ministering to the LORD in the presence of Eli. And the word of the LORD was rare in those days; there was no frequent vision.

²At that time Eli, whose eyesight had begun to grow dim so that he could not see, was lying down in his own place. ³The lamp of God had not yet gone out, and Samuel was lying down in the temple of the LORD, where the ark of God was.

⁴Then the LORD called Samuel, and he said, "Here I am!" ⁵and ran to Eli and said, "Here I am, for you called me." But he said, "I did not call; lie down again." So he went and lay down.

⁶And the LORD called again, "Samuel!" and Samuel arose and went to Eli and said, "Here I am, for you called me." But he

said, "I did not call, my son; lie down again." ⁷ Now Samuel did not yet know the LORD, and the word of the LORD had not yet been revealed to him.

⁸ And the LORD called Samuel again the third time. And he arose and went to Eli and said, "Here I am, for you called me." Then Eli perceived that the LORD was calling the boy. ⁹ Therefore Eli said to Samuel, "Go, lie down, and if he calls you, you shall say, 'Speak, LORD, for your servant hears.'" So Samuel went and lay down in his place.

¹⁰ And the LORD came and stood, calling as at other times, "Samuel! Samuel!" And Samuel said, "Speak, for your servant hears." ¹¹ Then the LORD said to Samuel, "Behold, I am about to do a thing in Israel at which the two ears of everyone who hears it will tingle. ¹² On that day I will fulfill against Eli all that I have spoken concerning his house, from beginning to end. ¹³ And I declare to him that I am about to punish his house forever, for the iniquity that he knew, because his sons were blaspheming God, and he did not restrain them. ¹⁴ Therefore I swear to the house of Eli that the iniquity of Eli's house shall not be atoned for by sacrifice or offering forever."

¹⁵ Samuel lay until morning; then he opened the doors of the house of the LORD. And Samuel was afraid to tell the vision to Eli. ¹⁶ But Eli called Samuel and said, "Samuel, my son." And he said, "Here I am." ¹⁷ And Eli said, "What was it that he told you? Do not hide it from me. May God do so to you and more also if you hide anything from me of all that he told you." ¹⁸ So Samuel told him everything and hid nothing from him. And he said, "It is the LORD. Let him do what seems good to him."

¹⁹ And Samuel grew, and the LORD was with him and let none of his words fall to the ground. ²⁰ And all Israel from Dan to

Beersheba knew that Samuel was established as a prophet of the LORD. ²¹ And the LORD appeared again at Shiloh, for the LORD revealed himself to Samuel at Shiloh by the word of the LORD.

The Philistines Capture the Ark

4 And the word of Samuel came to all Israel.

Now Israel went out to battle against the Philistines. They encamped at Ebenezer, and the Philistines encamped at Aphek. ² The Philistines drew up in line against Israel, and when the battle spread, Israel was defeated before the Philistines, who killed about four thousand men on the field of battle. ³ And when the people came to the camp, the elders of Israel said, "Why has the LORD defeated us today before the Philistines? Let us bring the ark of the covenant of the LORD here from Shiloh, that it may come among us and save us from the power of our enemies." ⁴ So the people sent to Shiloh and brought from there the ark of the covenant of the LORD of hosts, who is enthroned on the cherubim. And the two sons of Eli, Hophni and Phinehas, were there with the ark of the covenant of God.

⁵ As soon as the ark of the covenant of the LORD came into the camp, all Israel gave a mighty shout, so that the earth resounded. ⁶ And when the Philistines heard the noise of the shouting, they said, "What does this great shouting in the camp of the Hebrews mean?" And when they learned that the ark of the LORD had come to the camp, ⁷ the Philistines were afraid, for they said, "A god has come into the camp." And they said, "Woe to us! For nothing like this has happened before. ⁸ Woe to us! Who can deliver us from the power of these mighty gods? These are the gods who struck the Egyptians with every sort of plague in the wilderness. ⁹ Take

courage, and be men, O Philistines, lest you become slaves to the Hebrews as they have been to you; be men and fight."

[10] So the Philistines fought, and Israel was defeated, and they fled, every man to his home. And there was a very great slaughter, for thirty thousand foot soldiers of Israel fell. [11] And the ark of God was captured, and the two sons of Eli, Hophni and Phinehas, died.

The Death of Eli

[12] A man of Benjamin ran from the battle line and came to Shiloh the same day, with his clothes torn and with dirt on his head. [13] When he arrived, Eli was sitting on his seat by the road watching, for his heart trembled for the ark of God. And when the man came into the city and told the news, all the city cried out. [14] When Eli heard the sound of the outcry, he said, "What is this uproar?" Then the man hurried and came and told Eli. [15] Now Eli was ninety-eight years old and his eyes were set so that he could not see. [16] And the man said to Eli, "I am he who has come from the battle; I fled from the battle today." And he said, "How did it go, my son?" [17] He who brought the news answered and said, "Israel has fled before the Philistines, and there has also been a great defeat among the people. Your two sons also, Hophni and Phinehas, are dead, and the ark of God has been captured." [18] As soon as he mentioned the ark of God, Eli fell over backward from his seat by the side of the gate, and his neck was broken and he died, for the man was old and heavy. He had judged Israel forty years.

[19] Now his daughter-in-law, the wife of Phinehas, was pregnant, about to give birth. And when she heard the news that the ark of God was captured, and that her father-in-law and

her husband were dead, she bowed and gave birth, for her pains came upon her. ²⁰ And about the time of her death the women attending her said to her, "Do not be afraid, for you have borne a son." But she did not answer or pay attention. ²¹ And she named the child Ichabod, saying, "The glory has departed from Israel!" because the ark of God had been captured and because of her father-in-law and her husband. ²² And she said, "The glory has departed from Israel, for the ark of God has been captured."

The Philistines and the Ark

5 When the Philistines captured the ark of God, they brought it from Ebenezer to Ashdod. ² Then the Philistines took the ark of God and brought it into the house of Dagon and set it up beside Dagon. ³ And when the people of Ashdod rose early the next day, behold, Dagon had fallen face downward on the ground before the ark of the LORD. So they took Dagon and put him back in his place. ⁴ But when they rose early on the next morning, behold, Dagon had fallen face downward on the ground before the ark of the LORD, and the head of Dagon and both his hands were lying cut off on the threshold. Only the trunk of Dagon was left to him. ⁵ This is why the priests of Dagon and all who enter the house of Dagon do not tread on the threshold of Dagon in Ashdod to this day.

⁶ The hand of the LORD was heavy against the people of Ashdod, and he terrified and afflicted them with tumors, both Ashdod and its territory. ⁷ And when the men of Ashdod saw how things were, they said, "The ark of the God of Israel must not remain with us, for his hand is hard against us and against Dagon our god." ⁸ So they sent and gathered together all the lords of the Philistines and said, "What shall we do with the ark

of the God of Israel?" They answered, "Let the ark of the God of Israel be brought around to Gath." So they brought the ark of the God of Israel there. ⁹ But after they had brought it around, the hand of the LORD was against the city, causing a very great panic, and he afflicted the men of the city, both young and old, so that tumors broke out on them. ¹⁰ So they sent the ark of God to Ekron. But as soon as the ark of God came to Ekron, the people of Ekron cried out, "They have brought around to us the ark of the God of Israel to kill us and our people." ¹¹ They sent therefore and gathered together all the lords of the Philistines and said, "Send away the ark of the God of Israel, and let it return to its own place, that it may not kill us and our people." For there was a deathly panic throughout the whole city. The hand of God was very heavy there. ¹² The men who did not die were struck with tumors, and the cry of the city went up to heaven.

The Ark Returned to Israel

6 The ark of the LORD was in the country of the Philistines seven months. ² And the Philistines called for the priests and the diviners and said, "What shall we do with the ark of the LORD? Tell us with what we shall send it to its place." ³ They said, "If you send away the ark of the God of Israel, do not send it empty, but by all means return him a guilt offering. Then you will be healed, and it will be known to you why his hand does not turn away from you." ⁴ And they said, "What is the guilt offering that we shall return to him?" They answered, "Five golden tumors and five golden mice, according to the number of the lords of the Philistines, for the same plague was on all of you and on your lords. ⁵ So you must make images of

your tumors and images of your mice that ravage the land, and give glory to the God of Israel. Perhaps he will lighten his hand from off you and your gods and your land. ⁶ Why should you harden your hearts as the Egyptians and Pharaoh hardened their hearts? After he had dealt severely with them, did they not send the people away, and they departed? ⁷ Now then, take and prepare a new cart and two milk cows on which there has never come a yoke, and yoke the cows to the cart, but take their calves home, away from them. ⁸ And take the ark of the LORD and place it on the cart and put in a box at its side the figures of gold, which you are returning to him as a guilt offering. Then send it off and let it go its way ⁹ and watch. If it goes up on the way to its own land, to Beth-shemesh, then it is he who has done us this great harm, but if not, then we shall know that it is not his hand that struck us; it happened to us by coincidence."

¹⁰ The men did so, and took two milk cows and yoked them to the cart and shut up their calves at home. ¹¹ And they put the ark of the LORD on the cart and the box with the golden mice and the images of their tumors. ¹² And the cows went straight in the direction of Beth-shemesh along one highway, lowing as they went. They turned neither to the right nor to the left, and the lords of the Philistines went after them as far as the border of Beth-shemesh. ¹³ Now the people of Beth-shemesh were reaping their wheat harvest in the valley. And when they lifted up their eyes and saw the ark, they rejoiced to see it. ¹⁴ The cart came into the field of Joshua of Beth-shemesh and stopped there. A great stone was there. And they split up the wood of the cart and offered the cows as a burnt offering to the LORD. ¹⁵ And the Levites took down the ark of the LORD and the box that was beside it, in which were the golden figures, and set them upon the great

stone. And the men of Beth-shemesh offered burnt offerings and sacrificed sacrifices on that day to the LORD. ¹⁶And when the five lords of the Philistines saw it, they returned that day to Ekron.

¹⁷These are the golden tumors that the Philistines returned as a guilt offering to the LORD: one for Ashdod, one for Gaza, one for Ashkelon, one for Gath, one for Ekron, ¹⁸and the golden mice, according to the number of all the cities of the Philistines belonging to the five lords, both fortified cities and unwalled villages. The great stone beside which they set down the ark of the LORD is a witness to this day in the field of Joshua of Beth-shemesh.

¹⁹And he struck some of the men of Beth-shemesh, because they looked upon the ark of the LORD. He struck seventy men of them, and the people mourned because the LORD had struck the people with a great blow. ²⁰Then the men of Beth-shemesh said, "Who is able to stand before the LORD, this holy God? And to whom shall he go up away from us?" ²¹So they sent messengers to the inhabitants of Kiriath-jearim, saying, "The Philistines have returned the ark of the LORD. Come down and take it up to you."

7 And the men of Kiriath-jearim came and took up the ark of the LORD and brought it to the house of Abinadab on the hill. And they consecrated his son Eleazar to have charge of the ark of the LORD. ²From the day that the ark was lodged at Kiriath-jearim, a long time passed, some twenty years, and all the house of Israel lamented after the LORD.

Samuel Judges Israel

³And Samuel said to all the house of Israel, "If you are returning to the LORD with all your heart, then put away the

foreign gods and the Ashtaroth from among you and direct your heart to the LORD and serve him only, and he will deliver you out of the hand of the Philistines." ⁴ So the people of Israel put away the Baals and the Ashtaroth, and they served the LORD only.

⁵ Then Samuel said, "Gather all Israel at Mizpah, and I will pray to the LORD for you." ⁶ So they gathered at Mizpah and drew water and poured it out before the LORD and fasted on that day and said there, "We have sinned against the LORD." And Samuel judged the people of Israel at Mizpah. ⁷ Now when the Philistines heard that the people of Israel had gathered at Mizpah, the lords of the Philistines went up against Israel. And when the people of Israel heard of it, they were afraid of the Philistines. ⁸ And the people of Israel said to Samuel, "Do not cease to cry out to the LORD our God for us, that he may save us from the hand of the Philistines." ⁹ So Samuel took a nursing lamb and offered it as a whole burnt offering to the LORD. And Samuel cried out to the LORD for Israel, and the LORD answered him. ¹⁰ As Samuel was offering up the burnt offering, the Philistines drew near to attack Israel. But the LORD thundered with a mighty sound that day against the Philistines and threw them into confusion, and they were defeated before Israel. ¹¹ And the men of Israel went out from Mizpah and pursued the Philistines and struck them, as far as below Beth-car.

¹² Then Samuel took a stone and set it up between Mizpah and Shen and called its name Ebenezer; for he said, "Till now the LORD has helped us." ¹³ So the Philistines were subdued and did not again enter the territory of Israel. And the hand of the LORD was against the Philistines all the days of Samuel. ¹⁴ The

cities that the Philistines had taken from Israel were restored to Israel, from Ekron to Gath, and Israel delivered their territory from the hand of the Philistines. There was peace also between Israel and the Amorites.

¹⁵ Samuel judged Israel all the days of his life. ¹⁶ And he went on a circuit year by year to Bethel, Gilgal, and Mizpah. And he judged Israel in all these places. ¹⁷ Then he would return to Ramah, for his home was there, and there also he judged Israel. And he built there an altar to the LORD.

Israel Demands a King

8 When Samuel became old, he made his sons judges over Israel. ² The name of his firstborn son was Joel, and the name of his second, Abijah; they were judges in Beersheba. ³ Yet his sons did not walk in his ways but turned aside after gain. They took bribes and perverted justice.

⁴ Then all the elders of Israel gathered together and came to Samuel at Ramah ⁵ and said to him, "Behold, you are old and your sons do not walk in your ways. Now appoint for us a king to judge us like all the nations." ⁶ But the thing displeased Samuel when they said, "Give us a king to judge us." And Samuel prayed to the LORD. ⁷ And the LORD said to Samuel, "Obey the voice of the people in all that they say to you, for they have not rejected you, but they have rejected me from being king over them. ⁸ According to all the deeds that they have done, from the day I brought them up out of Egypt even to this day, forsaking me and serving other gods, so they are also doing to you. ⁹ Now then, obey their voice; only you shall solemnly warn them and show them the ways of the king who shall reign over them."

Samuel's Warning Against Kings

¹⁰ So Samuel told all the words of the LORD to the people who were asking for a king from him. ¹¹ He said, "These will be the ways of the king who will reign over you: he will take your sons and appoint them to his chariots and to be his horsemen and to run before his chariots. ¹² And he will appoint for himself commanders of thousands and commanders of fifties, and some to plow his ground and to reap his harvest, and to make his implements of war and the equipment of his chariots. ¹³ He will take your daughters to be perfumers and cooks and bakers. ¹⁴ He will take the best of your fields and vineyards and olive orchards and give them to his servants. ¹⁵ He will take the tenth of your grain and of your vineyards and give it to his officers and to his servants. ¹⁶ He will take your male servants and female servants and the best of your young men and your donkeys, and put them to his work. ¹⁷ He will take the tenth of your flocks, and you shall be his slaves. ¹⁸ And in that day you will cry out because of your king, whom you have chosen for yourselves, but the LORD will not answer you in that day."

The LORD Grants Israel's Request

¹⁹ But the people refused to obey the voice of Samuel. And they said, "No! But there shall be a king over us, ²⁰ that we also may be like all the nations, and that our king may judge us and go out before us and fight our battles." ²¹ And when Samuel had heard all the words of the people, he repeated them in the ears of the LORD. ²² And the LORD said to Samuel, "Obey their voice and make them a king." Samuel then said to the men of Israel, "Go every man to his city."

Saul Chosen to Be King

9 There was a man of Benjamin whose name was Kish, the son of Abiel, son of Zeror, son of Becorath, son of Aphiah, a Benjaminite, a man of wealth. ²And he had a son whose name was Saul, a handsome young man. There was not a man among the people of Israel more handsome than he. From his shoulders upward he was taller than any of the people.

³Now the donkeys of Kish, Saul's father, were lost. So Kish said to Saul his son, "Take one of the young men with you, and arise, go and look for the donkeys." ⁴And he passed through the hill country of Ephraim and passed through the land of Shalishah, but they did not find them. And they passed through the land of Shaalim, but they were not there. Then they passed through the land of Benjamin, but did not find them.

⁵When they came to the land of Zuph, Saul said to his servant who was with him, "Come, let us go back, lest my father cease to care about the donkeys and become anxious about us." ⁶But he said to him, "Behold, there is a man of God in this city, and he is a man who is held in honor; all that he says comes true. So now let us go there. Perhaps he can tell us the way we should go." ⁷Then Saul said to his servant, "But if we go, what can we bring the man? For the bread in our sacks is gone, and there is no present to bring to the man of God. What do we have?" ⁸The servant answered Saul again, "Here, I have with me a quarter of a shekel of silver, and I will give it to the man of God to tell us our way." ⁹(Formerly in Israel, when a man went to inquire of God, he said, "Come, let us go to the seer," for today's "prophet" was formerly called a seer.) ¹⁰And Saul said to his servant, "Well said; come, let us go." So they went to the city where the man of God was.

¹¹ As they went up the hill to the city, they met young women coming out to draw water and said to them, "Is the seer here?" ¹² They answered, "He is; behold, he is just ahead of you. Hurry. He has come just now to the city, because the people have a sacrifice today on the high place. ¹³ As soon as you enter the city you will find him, before he goes up to the high place to eat. For the people will not eat till he comes, since he must bless the sacrifice; afterward those who are invited will eat. Now go up, for you will meet him immediately." ¹⁴ So they went up to the city. As they were entering the city, they saw Samuel coming out toward them on his way up to the high place.

¹⁵ Now the day before Saul came, the LORD had revealed to Samuel: ¹⁶ "Tomorrow about this time I will send to you a man from the land of Benjamin, and you shall anoint him to be prince over my people Israel. He shall save my people from the hand of the Philistines. For I have seen my people, because their cry has come to me." ¹⁷ When Samuel saw Saul, the LORD told him, "Here is the man of whom I spoke to you! He it is who shall restrain my people." ¹⁸ Then Saul approached Samuel in the gate and said, "Tell me where is the house of the seer?" ¹⁹ Samuel answered Saul, "I am the seer. Go up before me to the high place, for today you shall eat with me, and in the morning I will let you go and will tell you all that is on your mind. ²⁰ As for your donkeys that were lost three days ago, do not set your mind on them, for they have been found. And for whom is all that is desirable in Israel? Is it not for you and for all your father's house?" ²¹ Saul answered, "Am I not a Benjaminite, from the least of the tribes of Israel? And is not my clan the humblest of all the clans of the tribe of Benjamin? Why then have you spoken to me in this way?"

²² Then Samuel took Saul and his young man and brought them into the hall and gave them a place at the head of those who had been invited, who were about thirty persons. ²³ And Samuel said to the cook, "Bring the portion I gave you, of which I said to you, 'Put it aside.'" ²⁴ So the cook took up the leg and what was on it and set them before Saul. And Samuel said, "See, what was kept is set before you. Eat, because it was kept for you until the hour appointed, that you might eat with the guests."

So Saul ate with Samuel that day. ²⁵ And when they came down from the high place into the city, a bed was spread for Saul on the roof, and he lay down to sleep. ²⁶ Then at the break of dawn Samuel called to Saul on the roof, "Up, that I may send you on your way." So Saul arose, and both he and Samuel went out into the street.

²⁷ As they were going down to the outskirts of the city, Samuel said to Saul, "Tell the servant to pass on before us, and when he has passed on, stop here yourself for a while, that I may make known to you the word of God."

Saul Anointed King

10 Then Samuel took a flask of oil and poured it on his head and kissed him and said, "Has not the LORD anointed you to be prince over his people Israel? And you shall reign over the people of the LORD and you will save them from the hand of their surrounding enemies. And this shall be the sign to you that the LORD has anointed you to be prince over his heritage. ² When you depart from me today, you will meet two men by Rachel's tomb in the territory of Benjamin at Zelzah, and they will say to you, 'The donkeys that you went to

seek are found, and now your father has ceased to care about the donkeys and is anxious about you, saying, "What shall I do about my son?" ' ³ Then you shall go on from there farther and come to the oak of Tabor. Three men going up to God at Bethel will meet you there, one carrying three young goats, another carrying three loaves of bread, and another carrying a skin of wine. ⁴ And they will greet you and give you two loaves of bread, which you shall accept from their hand. ⁵ After that you shall come to Gibeath-elohim, where there is a garrison of the Philistines. And there, as soon as you come to the city, you will meet a group of prophets coming down from the high place with harp, tambourine, flute, and lyre before them, prophesying. ⁶ Then the Spirit of the LORD will rush upon you, and you will prophesy with them and be turned into another man. ⁷ Now when these signs meet you, do what your hand finds to do, for God is with you. ⁸ Then go down before me to Gilgal. And behold, I am coming down to you to offer burnt offerings and to sacrifice peace offerings. Seven days you shall wait, until I come to you and show you what you shall do."

⁹ When he turned his back to leave Samuel, God gave him another heart. And all these signs came to pass that day. ¹⁰ When they came to Gibeah, behold, a group of prophets met him, and the Spirit of God rushed upon him, and he prophesied among them. ¹¹ And when all who knew him previously saw how he prophesied with the prophets, the people said to one another, "What has come over the son of Kish? Is Saul also among the prophets?" ¹² And a man of the place answered, "And who is their father?" Therefore it became a proverb, "Is Saul also among the prophets?" ¹³ When he had finished prophesying, he came to the high place.

¹⁴ Saul's uncle said to him and to his servant, "Where did you go?" And he said, "To seek the donkeys. And when we saw they were not to be found, we went to Samuel." ¹⁵ And Saul's uncle said, "Please tell me what Samuel said to you." ¹⁶ And Saul said to his uncle, "He told us plainly that the donkeys had been found." But about the matter of the kingdom, of which Samuel had spoken, he did not tell him anything.

Saul Proclaimed King

¹⁷ Now Samuel called the people together to the LORD at Mizpah. ¹⁸ And he said to the people of Israel, "Thus says the LORD, the God of Israel, 'I brought up Israel out of Egypt, and I delivered you from the hand of the Egyptians and from the hand of all the kingdoms that were oppressing you.' ¹⁹ But today you have rejected your God, who saves you from all your calamities and your distresses, and you have said to him, 'Set a king over us.' Now therefore present yourselves before the LORD by your tribes and by your thousands."

²⁰ Then Samuel brought all the tribes of Israel near, and the tribe of Benjamin was taken by lot. ²¹ He brought the tribe of Benjamin near by its clans, and the clan of the Matrites was taken by lot; and Saul the son of Kish was taken by lot. But when they sought him, he could not be found. ²² So they inquired again of the LORD, "Is there a man still to come?" and the LORD said, "Behold, he has hidden himself among the baggage." ²³ Then they ran and took him from there. And when he stood among the people, he was taller than any of the people from his shoulders upward. ²⁴ And Samuel said to all the people, "Do you see him whom the LORD has chosen? There is none like him among all the people." And all the people shouted, "Long live the king!"

²⁵ Then Samuel told the people the rights and duties of the kingship, and he wrote them in a book and laid it up before the LORD. Then Samuel sent all the people away, each one to his home. ²⁶ Saul also went to his home at Gibeah, and with him went men of valor whose hearts God had touched. ²⁷ But some worthless fellows said, "How can this man save us?" And they despised him and brought him no present. But he held his peace.

Saul Defeats the Ammonites

11 Then Nahash the Ammonite went up and besieged Jabesh-gilead, and all the men of Jabesh said to Nahash, "Make a treaty with us, and we will serve you." ² But Nahash the Ammonite said to them, "On this condition I will make a treaty with you, that I gouge out all your right eyes, and thus bring disgrace on all Israel." ³ The elders of Jabesh said to him, "Give us seven days' respite that we may send messengers through all the territory of Israel. Then, if there is no one to save us, we will give ourselves up to you." ⁴ When the messengers came to Gibeah of Saul, they reported the matter in the ears of the people, and all the people wept aloud.

⁵ Now, behold, Saul was coming from the field behind the oxen. And Saul said, "What is wrong with the people, that they are weeping?" So they told him the news of the men of Jabesh. ⁶ And the Spirit of God rushed upon Saul when he heard these words, and his anger was greatly kindled. ⁷ He took a yoke of oxen and cut them in pieces and sent them throughout all the territory of Israel by the hand of the messengers, saying, "Whoever does not come out after Saul and Samuel, so shall it be done to his oxen!" Then the dread of the LORD fell upon

the people, and they came out as one man. ⁸When he mustered them at Bezek, the people of Israel were three hundred thousand, and the men of Judah thirty thousand. ⁹And they said to the messengers who had come, "Thus shall you say to the men of Jabesh-gilead: 'Tomorrow, by the time the sun is hot, you shall have salvation.'" When the messengers came and told the men of Jabesh, they were glad. ¹⁰Therefore the men of Jabesh said, "Tomorrow we will give ourselves up to you, and you may do to us whatever seems good to you." ¹¹And the next day Saul put the people in three companies. And they came into the midst of the camp in the morning watch and struck down the Ammonites until the heat of the day. And those who survived were scattered, so that no two of them were left together.

The Kingdom Is Renewed

¹²Then the people said to Samuel, "Who is it that said, 'Shall Saul reign over us?' Bring the men, that we may put them to death." ¹³But Saul said, "Not a man shall be put to death this day, for today the LORD has worked salvation in Israel." ¹⁴Then Samuel said to the people, "Come, let us go to Gilgal and there renew the kingdom." ¹⁵So all the people went to Gilgal, and there they made Saul king before the LORD in Gilgal. There they sacrificed peace offerings before the LORD, and there Saul and all the men of Israel rejoiced greatly.

Samuel's Farewell Address

12 And Samuel said to all Israel, "Behold, I have obeyed your voice in all that you have said to me and have made a king over you. ²And now, behold, the king walks before you, and I am old and gray; and behold, my sons are with you. I have

walked before you from my youth until this day. ³ Here I am; testify against me before the LORD and before his anointed. Whose ox have I taken? Or whose donkey have I taken? Or whom have I defrauded? Whom have I oppressed? Or from whose hand have I taken a bribe to blind my eyes with it? Testify against me and I will restore it to you." ⁴ They said, "You have not defrauded us or oppressed us or taken anything from any man's hand." ⁵ And he said to them, "The LORD is witness against you, and his anointed is witness this day, that you have not found anything in my hand." And they said, "He is witness."

⁶ And Samuel said to the people, "The LORD is witness, who appointed Moses and Aaron and brought your fathers up out of the land of Egypt. ⁷ Now therefore stand still that I may plead with you before the LORD concerning all the righteous deeds of the LORD that he performed for you and for your fathers. ⁸ When Jacob went into Egypt, and the Egyptians oppressed them, then your fathers cried out to the LORD and the LORD sent Moses and Aaron, who brought your fathers out of Egypt and made them dwell in this place. ⁹ But they forgot the LORD their God. And he sold them into the hand of Sisera, commander of the army of Hazor, and into the hand of the Philistines, and into the hand of the king of Moab. And they fought against them. ¹⁰ And they cried out to the LORD and said, 'We have sinned, because we have forsaken the LORD and have served the Baals and the Ashtaroth. But now deliver us out of the hand of our enemies, that we may serve you.' ¹¹ And the LORD sent Jerubbaal and Barak and Jephthah and Samuel and delivered you out of the hand of your enemies on every side, and you lived in safety. ¹² And when you saw that Nahash the king of the Ammonites came against you, you said to me, 'No, but a king shall reign

over us,' when the LORD your God was your king. ¹³ And now behold the king whom you have chosen, for whom you have asked; behold, the LORD has set a king over you. ¹⁴ If you will fear the LORD and serve him and obey his voice and not rebel against the commandment of the LORD, and if both you and the king who reigns over you will follow the LORD your God, it will be well. ¹⁵ But if you will not obey the voice of the LORD, but rebel against the commandment of the LORD, then the hand of the LORD will be against you and your king. ¹⁶ Now therefore stand still and see this great thing that the LORD will do before your eyes. ¹⁷ Is it not wheat harvest today? I will call upon the LORD, that he may send thunder and rain. And you shall know and see that your wickedness is great, which you have done in the sight of the LORD, in asking for yourselves a king." ¹⁸ So Samuel called upon the LORD, and the LORD sent thunder and rain that day, and all the people greatly feared the LORD and Samuel.

¹⁹ And all the people said to Samuel, "Pray for your servants to the LORD your God, that we may not die, for we have added to all our sins this evil, to ask for ourselves a king." ²⁰ And Samuel said to the people, "Do not be afraid; you have done all this evil. Yet do not turn aside from following the LORD, but serve the LORD with all your heart. ²¹ And do not turn aside after empty things that cannot profit or deliver, for they are empty. ²² For the LORD will not forsake his people, for his great name's sake, because it has pleased the LORD to make you a people for himself. ²³ Moreover, as for me, far be it from me that I should sin against the LORD by ceasing to pray for you, and I will instruct you in the good and the right way. ²⁴ Only fear the LORD and serve him faithfully with all your heart. For consider what great

things he has done for you. [25] But if you still do wickedly, you shall be swept away, both you and your king."

Saul Fights the Philistines

13 Saul lived for one year and then became king, and when he had reigned for two years over Israel, [2] Saul chose three thousand men of Israel. Two thousand were with Saul in Michmash and the hill country of Bethel, and a thousand were with Jonathan in Gibeah of Benjamin. The rest of the people he sent home, every man to his tent. [3] Jonathan defeated the garrison of the Philistines that was at Geba, and the Philistines heard of it. And Saul blew the trumpet throughout all the land, saying, "Let the Hebrews hear." [4] And all Israel heard it said that Saul had defeated the garrison of the Philistines, and also that Israel had become a stench to the Philistines. And the people were called out to join Saul at Gilgal.

[5] And the Philistines mustered to fight with Israel, thirty thousand chariots and six thousand horsemen and troops like the sand on the seashore in multitude. They came up and encamped in Michmash, to the east of Beth-aven. [6] When the men of Israel saw that they were in trouble (for the people were hard pressed), the people hid themselves in caves and in holes and in rocks and in tombs and in cisterns, [7] and some Hebrews crossed the fords of the Jordan to the land of Gad and Gilead. Saul was still at Gilgal, and all the people followed him trembling.

Saul's Unlawful Sacrifice

[8] He waited seven days, the time appointed by Samuel. But Samuel did not come to Gilgal, and the people were scattering from him. [9] So Saul said, "Bring the burnt offering here to

me, and the peace offerings." And he offered the burnt offering. ¹⁰ As soon as he had finished offering the burnt offering, behold, Samuel came. And Saul went out to meet him and greet him. ¹¹ Samuel said, "What have you done?" And Saul said, "When I saw that the people were scattering from me, and that you did not come within the days appointed, and that the Philistines had mustered at Michmash, ¹² I said, 'Now the Philistines will come down against me at Gilgal, and I have not sought the favor of the LORD.' So I forced myself, and offered the burnt offering." ¹³ And Samuel said to Saul, "You have done foolishly. You have not kept the command of the LORD your God, with which he commanded you. For then the LORD would have established your kingdom over Israel forever. ¹⁴ But now your kingdom shall not continue. The LORD has sought out a man after his own heart, and the LORD has commanded him to be prince over his people, because you have not kept what the LORD commanded you." ¹⁵ And Samuel arose and went up from Gilgal. The rest of the people went up after Saul to meet the army; they went up from Gilgal to Gibeah of Benjamin.

And Saul numbered the people who were present with him, about six hundred men. ¹⁶ And Saul and Jonathan his son and the people who were present with them stayed in Geba of Benjamin, but the Philistines encamped in Michmash. ¹⁷ And raiders came out of the camp of the Philistines in three companies. One company turned toward Ophrah, to the land of Shual; ¹⁸ another company turned toward Beth-horon; and another company turned toward the border that looks down on the Valley of Zeboim toward the wilderness.

¹⁹ Now there was no blacksmith to be found throughout all the land of Israel, for the Philistines said, "Lest the Hebrews

make themselves swords or spears." ²⁰ But every one of the Israelites went down to the Philistines to sharpen his plowshare, his mattock, his axe, or his sickle, ²¹ and the charge was two-thirds of a shekel for the plowshares and for the mattocks, and a third of a shekel for sharpening the axes and for setting the goads. ²² So on the day of the battle there was neither sword nor spear found in the hand of any of the people with Saul and Jonathan, but Saul and Jonathan his son had them. ²³ And the garrison of the Philistines went out to the pass of Michmash.

Jonathan Defeats the Philistines

14 One day Jonathan the son of Saul said to the young man who carried his armor, "Come, let us go over to the Philistine garrison on the other side." But he did not tell his father. ² Saul was staying in the outskirts of Gibeah in the pomegranate cave at Migron. The people who were with him were about six hundred men, ³ including Ahijah the son of Ahitub, Ichabod's brother, son of Phinehas, son of Eli, the priest of the LORD in Shiloh, wearing an ephod. And the people did not know that Jonathan had gone. ⁴ Within the passes, by which Jonathan sought to go over to the Philistine garrison, there was a rocky crag on the one side and a rocky crag on the other side. The name of the one was Bozez, and the name of the other Seneh. ⁵ The one crag rose on the north in front of Michmash, and the other on the south in front of Geba.

⁶ Jonathan said to the young man who carried his armor, "Come, let us go over to the garrison of these uncircumcised. It may be that the LORD will work for us, for nothing can hinder the LORD from saving by many or by few." ⁷ And his armorbearer said to him, "Do all that is in your heart. Do as you wish.

Behold, I am with you heart and soul." ⁸ Then Jonathan said, "Behold, we will cross over to the men, and we will show ourselves to them. ⁹ If they say to us, 'Wait until we come to you,' then we will stand still in our place, and we will not go up to them. ¹⁰ But if they say, 'Come up to us,' then we will go up, for the LORD has given them into our hand. And this shall be the sign to us." ¹¹ So both of them showed themselves to the garrison of the Philistines. And the Philistines said, "Look, Hebrews are coming out of the holes where they have hidden themselves." ¹² And the men of the garrison hailed Jonathan and his armor-bearer and said, "Come up to us, and we will show you a thing." And Jonathan said to his armor-bearer, "Come up after me, for the LORD has given them into the hand of Israel." ¹³ Then Jonathan climbed up on his hands and feet, and his armor-bearer after him. And they fell before Jonathan, and his armor-bearer killed them after him. ¹⁴ And that first strike, which Jonathan and his armor-bearer made, killed about twenty men within as it were half a furrow's length in an acre of land. ¹⁵ And there was a panic in the camp, in the field, and among all the people. The garrison and even the raiders trembled, the earth quaked, and it became a very great panic.

¹⁶ And the watchmen of Saul in Gibeah of Benjamin looked, and behold, the multitude was dispersing here and there. ¹⁷ Then Saul said to the people who were with him, "Count and see who has gone from us." And when they had counted, behold, Jonathan and his armor-bearer were not there. ¹⁸ So Saul said to Ahijah, "Bring the ark of God here." For the ark of God went at that time with the people of Israel. ¹⁹ Now while Saul was talking to the priest, the tumult in the camp of the Philistines increased more and more. So Saul said to the priest, "Withdraw

your hand." ²⁰ Then Saul and all the people who were with him rallied and went into the battle. And behold, every Philistine's sword was against his fellow, and there was very great confusion. ²¹ Now the Hebrews who had been with the Philistines before that time and who had gone up with them into the camp, even they also turned to be with the Israelites who were with Saul and Jonathan. ²² Likewise, when all the men of Israel who had hidden themselves in the hill country of Ephraim heard that the Philistines were fleeing, they too followed hard after them in the battle. ²³ So the LORD saved Israel that day. And the battle passed beyond Beth-aven.

Saul's Rash Vow

²⁴ And the men of Israel had been hard pressed that day, so Saul had laid an oath on the people, saying, "Cursed be the man who eats food until it is evening and I am avenged on my enemies." So none of the people had tasted food. ²⁵ Now when all the people came to the forest, behold, there was honey on the ground. ²⁶ And when the people entered the forest, behold, the honey was dropping, but no one put his hand to his mouth, for the people feared the oath. ²⁷ But Jonathan had not heard his father charge the people with the oath, so he put out the tip of the staff that was in his hand and dipped it in the honeycomb and put his hand to his mouth, and his eyes became bright. ²⁸ Then one of the people said, "Your father strictly charged the people with an oath, saying, 'Cursed be the man who eats food this day.'" And the people were faint. ²⁹ Then Jonathan said, "My father has troubled the land. See how my eyes have become bright because I tasted a little of this honey. ³⁰ How much better if the people had eaten freely today of the spoil of

their enemies that they found. For now the defeat among the Philistines has not been great."

³¹ They struck down the Philistines that day from Michmash to Aijalon. And the people were very faint. ³² The people pounced on the spoil and took sheep and oxen and calves and slaughtered them on the ground. And the people ate them with the blood. ³³ Then they told Saul, "Behold, the people are sinning against the LORD by eating with the blood." And he said, "You have dealt treacherously; roll a great stone to me here." ³⁴ And Saul said, "Disperse yourselves among the people and say to them, 'Let every man bring his ox or his sheep and slaughter them here and eat, and do not sin against the LORD by eating with the blood.'" So every one of the people brought his ox with him that night and they slaughtered them there. ³⁵ And Saul built an altar to the LORD; it was the first altar that he built to the LORD.

³⁶ Then Saul said, "Let us go down after the Philistines by night and plunder them until the morning light; let us not leave a man of them." And they said, "Do whatever seems good to you." But the priest said, "Let us draw near to God here." ³⁷ And Saul inquired of God, "Shall I go down after the Philistines? Will you give them into the hand of Israel?" But he did not answer him that day. ³⁸ And Saul said, "Come here, all you leaders of the people, and know and see how this sin has arisen today. ³⁹ For as the LORD lives who saves Israel, though it be in Jonathan my son, he shall surely die." But there was not a man among all the people who answered him. ⁴⁰ Then he said to all Israel, "You shall be on one side, and I and Jonathan my son will be on the other side." And the people said to Saul, "Do what seems good to you." ⁴¹ Therefore Saul said, "O LORD

God of Israel, why have you not answered your servant this day? If this guilt is in me or in Jonathan my son, O LORD, God of Israel, give Urim. But if this guilt is in your people Israel, give Thummim." And Jonathan and Saul were taken, but the people escaped. ⁴²Then Saul said, "Cast the lot between me and my son Jonathan." And Jonathan was taken.

⁴³ Then Saul said to Jonathan, "Tell me what you have done." And Jonathan told him, "I tasted a little honey with the tip of the staff that was in my hand. Here I am; I will die." ⁴⁴And Saul said, "God do so to me and more also; you shall surely die, Jonathan." ⁴⁵Then the people said to Saul, "Shall Jonathan die, who has worked this great salvation in Israel? Far from it! As the LORD lives, there shall not one hair of his head fall to the ground, for he has worked with God this day." So the people ransomed Jonathan, so that he did not die. ⁴⁶Then Saul went up from pursuing the Philistines, and the Philistines went to their own place.

Saul Fights Israel's Enemies

⁴⁷When Saul had taken the kingship over Israel, he fought against all his enemies on every side, against Moab, against the Ammonites, against Edom, against the kings of Zobah, and against the Philistines. Wherever he turned he routed them. ⁴⁸And he did valiantly and struck the Amalekites and delivered Israel out of the hands of those who plundered them.

⁴⁹Now the sons of Saul were Jonathan, Ishvi, and Malchishua. And the names of his two daughters were these: the name of the firstborn was Merab, and the name of the younger Michal. ⁵⁰And the name of Saul's wife was Ahinoam the daughter of Ahimaaz. And the name of the commander of his army

was Abner the son of Ner, Saul's uncle. [51] Kish was the father of Saul, and Ner the father of Abner was the son of Abiel.

[52] There was hard fighting against the Philistines all the days of Saul. And when Saul saw any strong man, or any valiant man, he attached him to himself.

The Lord Rejects Saul

15 And Samuel said to Saul, "The Lord sent me to anoint you king over his people Israel; now therefore listen to the words of the Lord. [2] Thus says the Lord of hosts, 'I have noted what Amalek did to Israel in opposing them on the way when they came up out of Egypt. [3] Now go and strike Amalek and devote to destruction all that they have. Do not spare them, but kill both man and woman, child and infant, ox and sheep, camel and donkey.'"

[4] So Saul summoned the people and numbered them in Telaim, two hundred thousand men on foot, and ten thousand men of Judah. [5] And Saul came to the city of Amalek and lay in wait in the valley. [6] Then Saul said to the Kenites, "Go, depart; go down from among the Amalekites, lest I destroy you with them. For you showed kindness to all the people of Israel when they came up out of Egypt." So the Kenites departed from among the Amalekites. [7] And Saul defeated the Amalekites from Havilah as far as Shur, which is east of Egypt. [8] And he took Agag the king of the Amalekites alive and devoted to destruction all the people with the edge of the sword. [9] But Saul and the people spared Agag and the best of the sheep and of the oxen and of the fattened calves and the lambs, and all that was good, and would not utterly destroy them. All that was despised and worthless they devoted to destruction.

¹⁰ The word of the LORD came to Samuel: ¹¹ "I regret that I have made Saul king, for he has turned back from following me and has not performed my commandments." And Samuel was angry, and he cried to the LORD all night. ¹² And Samuel rose early to meet Saul in the morning. And it was told Samuel, "Saul came to Carmel, and behold, he set up a monument for himself and turned and passed on and went down to Gilgal." ¹³ And Samuel came to Saul, and Saul said to him, "Blessed be you to the LORD. I have performed the commandment of the LORD." ¹⁴ And Samuel said, "What then is this bleating of the sheep in my ears and the lowing of the oxen that I hear?" ¹⁵ Saul said, "They have brought them from the Amalekites, for the people spared the best of the sheep and of the oxen to sacrifice to the LORD your God, and the rest we have devoted to destruction." ¹⁶ Then Samuel said to Saul, "Stop! I will tell you what the LORD said to me this night." And he said to him, "Speak."

¹⁷ And Samuel said, "Though you are little in your own eyes, are you not the head of the tribes of Israel? The LORD anointed you king over Israel. ¹⁸ And the LORD sent you on a mission and said, 'Go, devote to destruction the sinners, the Amalekites, and fight against them until they are consumed.' ¹⁹ Why then did you not obey the voice of the LORD? Why did you pounce on the spoil and do what was evil in the sight of the LORD?" ²⁰ And Saul said to Samuel, "I have obeyed the voice of the LORD. I have gone on the mission on which the LORD sent me. I have brought Agag the king of Amalek, and I have devoted the Amalekites to destruction. ²¹ But the people took of the spoil, sheep and oxen, the best of the things devoted to destruction, to sacrifice to the LORD your God in Gilgal." ²² And Samuel said,

"Has the LORD as great delight in burnt offerings and
       sacrifices,
    as in obeying the voice of the LORD?
Behold, to obey is better than sacrifice,
    and to listen than the fat of rams.
23   For rebellion is as the sin of divination,
    and presumption is as iniquity and idolatry.
Because you have rejected the word of the LORD,
    he has also rejected you from being king."

²⁴ Saul said to Samuel, "I have sinned, for I have transgressed
the commandment of the LORD and your words, because I
feared the people and obeyed their voice. ²⁵ Now therefore,
please pardon my sin and return with me that I may bow before
the LORD." ²⁶ And Samuel said to Saul, "I will not return with
you. For you have rejected the word of the LORD, and the LORD
has rejected you from being king over Israel." ²⁷ As Samuel
turned to go away, Saul seized the skirt of his robe, and it tore.
²⁸ And Samuel said to him, "The LORD has torn the kingdom of
Israel from you this day and has given it to a neighbor of yours,
who is better than you. ²⁹ And also the Glory of Israel will not lie
or have regret, for he is not a man, that he should have regret."
³⁰ Then he said, "I have sinned; yet honor me now before the
elders of my people and before Israel, and return with me, that
I may bow before the LORD your God." ³¹ So Samuel turned
back after Saul, and Saul bowed before the LORD.

³² Then Samuel said, "Bring here to me Agag the king of
the Amalekites." And Agag came to him cheerfully. Agag said,
"Surely the bitterness of death is past." ³³ And Samuel said, "As
your sword has made women childless, so shall your mother be

childless among women." And Samuel hacked Agag to pieces before the LORD in Gilgal.

³⁴ Then Samuel went to Ramah, and Saul went up to his house in Gibeah of Saul. ³⁵ And Samuel did not see Saul again until the day of his death, but Samuel grieved over Saul. And the LORD regretted that he had made Saul king over Israel.

David Anointed King

16 The LORD said to Samuel, "How long will you grieve over Saul, since I have rejected him from being king over Israel? Fill your horn with oil, and go. I will send you to Jesse the Bethlehemite, for I have provided for myself a king among his sons." ² And Samuel said, "How can I go? If Saul hears it, he will kill me." And the LORD said, "Take a heifer with you and say, 'I have come to sacrifice to the LORD.' ³ And invite Jesse to the sacrifice, and I will show you what you shall do. And you shall anoint for me him whom I declare to you." ⁴ Samuel did what the LORD commanded and came to Bethlehem. The elders of the city came to meet him trembling and said, "Do you come peaceably?" ⁵ And he said, "Peaceably; I have come to sacrifice to the LORD. Consecrate yourselves, and come with me to the sacrifice." And he consecrated Jesse and his sons and invited them to the sacrifice.

⁶ When they came, he looked on Eliab and thought, "Surely the LORD's anointed is before him." ⁷ But the LORD said to Samuel, "Do not look on his appearance or on the height of his stature, because I have rejected him. For the LORD sees not as man sees: man looks on the outward appearance, but the LORD looks on the heart." ⁸ Then Jesse called Abinadab and made him pass before Samuel. And he said, "Neither has the LORD chosen

this one." ⁹ Then Jesse made Shammah pass by. And he said, "Neither has the LORD chosen this one." ¹⁰ And Jesse made seven of his sons pass before Samuel. And Samuel said to Jesse, "The LORD has not chosen these." ¹¹ Then Samuel said to Jesse, "Are all your sons here?" And he said, "There remains yet the youngest, but behold, he is keeping the sheep." And Samuel said to Jesse, "Send and get him, for we will not sit down till he comes here." ¹² And he sent and brought him in. Now he was ruddy and had beautiful eyes and was handsome. And the LORD said, "Arise, anoint him, for this is he." ¹³ Then Samuel took the horn of oil and anointed him in the midst of his brothers. And the Spirit of the LORD rushed upon David from that day forward. And Samuel rose up and went to Ramah.

David in Saul's Service

¹⁴ Now the Spirit of the LORD departed from Saul, and a harmful spirit from the LORD tormented him. ¹⁵ And Saul's servants said to him, "Behold now, a harmful spirit from God is tormenting you. ¹⁶ Let our lord now command your servants who are before you to seek out a man who is skillful in playing the lyre, and when the harmful spirit from God is upon you, he will play it, and you will be well." ¹⁷ So Saul said to his servants, "Provide for me a man who can play well and bring him to me." ¹⁸ One of the young men answered, "Behold, I have seen a son of Jesse the Bethlehemite, who is skillful in playing, a man of valor, a man of war, prudent in speech, and a man of good presence, and the LORD is with him." ¹⁹ Therefore Saul sent messengers to Jesse and said, "Send me David your son, who is with the sheep." ²⁰ And Jesse took a donkey laden with bread and a skin of wine and a young goat and sent them by David his son

to Saul. ²¹ And David came to Saul and entered his service. And Saul loved him greatly, and he became his armor-bearer. ²² And Saul sent to Jesse, saying, "Let David remain in my service, for he has found favor in my sight." ²³ And whenever the harmful spirit from God was upon Saul, David took the lyre and played it with his hand. So Saul was refreshed and was well, and the harmful spirit departed from him.

David and Goliath

17 Now the Philistines gathered their armies for battle. And they were gathered at Socoh, which belongs to Judah, and encamped between Socoh and Azekah, in Ephes-dammim. ² And Saul and the men of Israel were gathered, and encamped in the Valley of Elah, and drew up in line of battle against the Philistines. ³ And the Philistines stood on the mountain on the one side, and Israel stood on the mountain on the other side, with a valley between them. ⁴ And there came out from the camp of the Philistines a champion named Goliath of Gath, whose height was six cubits and a span. ⁵ He had a helmet of bronze on his head, and he was armed with a coat of mail, and the weight of the coat was five thousand shekels of bronze. ⁶ And he had bronze armor on his legs, and a javelin of bronze slung between his shoulders. ⁷ The shaft of his spear was like a weaver's beam, and his spear's head weighed six hundred shekels of iron. And his shield-bearer went before him. ⁸ He stood and shouted to the ranks of Israel, "Why have you come out to draw up for battle? Am I not a Philistine, and are you not servants of Saul? Choose a man for yourselves, and let him come down to me. ⁹ If he is able to fight with me and kill me, then we will be your servants. But if I prevail against him and kill

him, then you shall be our servants and serve us." **10** And the Philistine said, "I defy the ranks of Israel this day. Give me a man, that we may fight together." **11** When Saul and all Israel heard these words of the Philistine, they were dismayed and greatly afraid.

12 Now David was the son of an Ephrathite of Bethlehem in Judah, named Jesse, who had eight sons. In the days of Saul the man was already old and advanced in years. **13** The three oldest sons of Jesse had followed Saul to the battle. And the names of his three sons who went to the battle were Eliab the firstborn, and next to him Abinadab, and the third Shammah. **14** David was the youngest. The three eldest followed Saul, **15** but David went back and forth from Saul to feed his father's sheep at Bethlehem. **16** For forty days the Philistine came forward and took his stand, morning and evening.

17 And Jesse said to David his son, "Take for your brothers an ephah of this parched grain, and these ten loaves, and carry them quickly to the camp to your brothers. **18** Also take these ten cheeses to the commander of their thousand. See if your brothers are well, and bring some token from them."

19 Now Saul and they and all the men of Israel were in the Valley of Elah, fighting with the Philistines. **20** And David rose early in the morning and left the sheep with a keeper and took the provisions and went, as Jesse had commanded him. And he came to the encampment as the host was going out to the battle line, shouting the war cry. **21** And Israel and the Philistines drew up for battle, army against army. **22** And David left the things in charge of the keeper of the baggage and ran to the ranks and went and greeted his brothers. **23** As he talked with them, behold, the champion, the Philistine of Gath, Goliath by

name, came up out of the ranks of the Philistines and spoke the same words as before. And David heard him.

²⁴ All the men of Israel, when they saw the man, fled from him and were much afraid. ²⁵ And the men of Israel said, "Have you seen this man who has come up? Surely he has come up to defy Israel. And the king will enrich the man who kills him with great riches and will give him his daughter and make his father's house free in Israel." ²⁶ And David said to the men who stood by him, "What shall be done for the man who kills this Philistine and takes away the reproach from Israel? For who is this uncircumcised Philistine, that he should defy the armies of the living God?" ²⁷ And the people answered him in the same way, "So shall it be done to the man who kills him."

²⁸ Now Eliab his eldest brother heard when he spoke to the men. And Eliab's anger was kindled against David, and he said, "Why have you come down? And with whom have you left those few sheep in the wilderness? I know your presumption and the evil of your heart, for you have come down to see the battle." ²⁹ And David said, "What have I done now? Was it not but a word?" ³⁰ And he turned away from him toward another, and spoke in the same way, and the people answered him again as before.

³¹ When the words that David spoke were heard, they repeated them before Saul, and he sent for him. ³² And David said to Saul, "Let no man's heart fail because of him. Your servant will go and fight with this Philistine." ³³ And Saul said to David, "You are not able to go against this Philistine to fight with him, for you are but a youth, and he has been a man of war from his youth." ³⁴ But David said to Saul, "Your servant used to keep sheep for his father. And when there came a lion, or a bear,

and took a lamb from the flock, ³⁵ I went after him and struck him and delivered it out of his mouth. And if he arose against me, I caught him by his beard and struck him and killed him. ³⁶ Your servant has struck down both lions and bears, and this uncircumcised Philistine shall be like one of them, for he has defied the armies of the living God." ³⁷ And David said, "The LORD who delivered me from the paw of the lion and from the paw of the bear will deliver me from the hand of this Philistine." And Saul said to David, "Go, and the LORD be with you!"

³⁸ Then Saul clothed David with his armor. He put a helmet of bronze on his head and clothed him with a coat of mail, ³⁹ and David strapped his sword over his armor. And he tried in vain to go, for he had not tested them. Then David said to Saul, "I cannot go with these, for I have not tested them." So David put them off. ⁴⁰ Then he took his staff in his hand and chose five smooth stones from the brook and put them in his shepherd's pouch. His sling was in his hand, and he approached the Philistine.

⁴¹ And the Philistine moved forward and came near to David, with his shield-bearer in front of him. ⁴² And when the Philistine looked and saw David, he disdained him, for he was but a youth, ruddy and handsome in appearance. ⁴³ And the Philistine said to David, "Am I a dog, that you come to me with sticks?" And the Philistine cursed David by his gods. ⁴⁴ The Philistine said to David, "Come to me, and I will give your flesh to the birds of the air and to the beasts of the field." ⁴⁵ Then David said to the Philistine, "You come to me with a sword and with a spear and with a javelin, but I come to you in the name of the LORD of hosts, the God of the armies of Israel, whom you have defied. ⁴⁶ This day the LORD will deliver you into my hand, and I will strike you down and cut off your head. And I will

give the dead bodies of the host of the Philistines this day to the birds of the air and to the wild beasts of the earth, that all the earth may know that there is a God in Israel, ⁴⁷ and that all this assembly may know that the LORD saves not with sword and spear. For the battle is the LORD's, and he will give you into our hand."

⁴⁸ When the Philistine arose and came and drew near to meet David, David ran quickly toward the battle line to meet the Philistine. ⁴⁹ And David put his hand in his bag and took out a stone and slung it and struck the Philistine on his forehead. The stone sank into his forehead, and he fell on his face to the ground.

⁵⁰ So David prevailed over the Philistine with a sling and with a stone, and struck the Philistine and killed him. There was no sword in the hand of David. ⁵¹ Then David ran and stood over the Philistine and took his sword and drew it out of its sheath and killed him and cut off his head with it. When the Philistines saw that their champion was dead, they fled. ⁵² And the men of Israel and Judah rose with a shout and pursued the Philistines as far as Gath and the gates of Ekron, so that the wounded Philistines fell on the way from Shaaraim as far as Gath and Ekron. ⁵³ And the people of Israel came back from chasing the Philistines, and they plundered their camp. ⁵⁴ And David took the head of the Philistine and brought it to Jerusalem, but he put his armor in his tent.

⁵⁵ As soon as Saul saw David go out against the Philistine, he said to Abner, the commander of the army, "Abner, whose son is this youth?" And Abner said, "As your soul lives, O king, I do not know." ⁵⁶ And the king said, "Inquire whose son the boy is." ⁵⁷ And as soon as David returned from the striking down of the

Philistine, Abner took him, and brought him before Saul with the head of the Philistine in his hand. [58] And Saul said to him, "Whose son are you, young man?" And David answered, "I am the son of your servant Jesse the Bethlehemite."

David and Jonathan's Friendship

18 As soon as he had finished speaking to Saul, the soul of Jonathan was knit to the soul of David, and Jonathan loved him as his own soul. [2] And Saul took him that day and would not let him return to his father's house. [3] Then Jonathan made a covenant with David, because he loved him as his own soul. [4] And Jonathan stripped himself of the robe that was on him and gave it to David, and his armor, and even his sword and his bow and his belt. [5] And David went out and was successful wherever Saul sent him, so that Saul set him over the men of war. And this was good in the sight of all the people and also in the sight of Saul's servants.

Saul's Jealousy of David

[6] As they were coming home, when David returned from striking down the Philistine, the women came out of all the cities of Israel, singing and dancing, to meet King Saul, with tambourines, with songs of joy, and with musical instruments. [7] And the women sang to one another as they celebrated,

> "Saul has struck down his thousands,
>   and David his ten thousands."

[8] And Saul was very angry, and this saying displeased him. He said, "They have ascribed to David ten thousands, and to me

they have ascribed thousands, and what more can he have but the kingdom?" ⁹And Saul eyed David from that day on.

¹⁰The next day a harmful spirit from God rushed upon Saul, and he raved within his house while David was playing the lyre, as he did day by day. Saul had his spear in his hand. ¹¹And Saul hurled the spear, for he thought, "I will pin David to the wall." But David evaded him twice.

¹²Saul was afraid of David because the Lᴏʀᴅ was with him but had departed from Saul. ¹³So Saul removed him from his presence and made him a commander of a thousand. And he went out and came in before the people. ¹⁴And David had success in all his undertakings, for the Lᴏʀᴅ was with him. ¹⁵And when Saul saw that he had great success, he stood in fearful awe of him. ¹⁶But all Israel and Judah loved David, for he went out and came in before them.

David Marries Michal

¹⁷ Then Saul said to David, "Here is my elder daughter Merab. I will give her to you for a wife. Only be valiant for me and fight the Lᴏʀᴅ's battles." For Saul thought, "Let not my hand be against him, but let the hand of the Philistines be against him." ¹⁸And David said to Saul, "Who am I, and who are my relatives, my father's clan in Israel, that I should be son-in-law to the king?" ¹⁹But at the time when Merab, Saul's daughter, should have been given to David, she was given to Adriel the Meholathite for a wife.

²⁰Now Saul's daughter Michal loved David. And they told Saul, and the thing pleased him. ²¹Saul thought, "Let me give her to him, that she may be a snare for him and that the hand of the Philistines may be against him." Therefore Saul said to

David a second time, "You shall now be my son-in-law." ²² And Saul commanded his servants, "Speak to David in private and say, 'Behold, the king has delight in you, and all his servants love you. Now then become the king's son-in-law.'" ²³ And Saul's servants spoke those words in the ears of David. And David said, "Does it seem to you a little thing to become the king's son-in-law, since I am a poor man and have no reputation?" ²⁴ And the servants of Saul told him, "Thus and so did David speak." ²⁵ Then Saul said, "Thus shall you say to David, 'The king desires no bride-price except a hundred foreskins of the Philistines, that he may be avenged of the king's enemies.'" Now Saul thought to make David fall by the hand of the Philistines. ²⁶ And when his servants told David these words, it pleased David well to be the king's son-in-law. Before the time had expired, ²⁷ David arose and went, along with his men, and killed two hundred of the Philistines. And David brought their foreskins, which were given in full number to the king, that he might become the king's son-in-law. And Saul gave him his daughter Michal for a wife. ²⁸ But when Saul saw and knew that the LORD was with David, and that Michal, Saul's daughter, loved him, ²⁹ Saul was even more afraid of David. So Saul was David's enemy continually.

³⁰ Then the commanders of the Philistines came out to battle, and as often as they came out David had more success than all the servants of Saul, so that his name was highly esteemed.

Saul Tries to Kill David

19 And Saul spoke to Jonathan his son and to all his servants, that they should kill David. But Jonathan, Saul's son, delighted much in David. ² And Jonathan told David, "Saul

my father seeks to kill you. Therefore be on your guard in the morning. Stay in a secret place and hide yourself. ³ And I will go out and stand beside my father in the field where you are, and I will speak to my father about you. And if I learn anything I will tell you." ⁴ And Jonathan spoke well of David to Saul his father and said to him, "Let not the king sin against his servant David, because he has not sinned against you, and because his deeds have brought good to you. ⁵ For he took his life in his hand and he struck down the Philistine, and the LORD worked a great salvation for all Israel. You saw it, and rejoiced. Why then will you sin against innocent blood by killing David without cause?" ⁶ And Saul listened to the voice of Jonathan. Saul swore, "As the LORD lives, he shall not be put to death." ⁷ And Jonathan called David, and Jonathan reported to him all these things. And Jonathan brought David to Saul, and he was in his presence as before.

⁸ And there was war again. And David went out and fought with the Philistines and struck them with a great blow, so that they fled before him. ⁹ Then a harmful spirit from the LORD came upon Saul, as he sat in his house with his spear in his hand. And David was playing the lyre. ¹⁰ And Saul sought to pin David to the wall with the spear, but he eluded Saul, so that he struck the spear into the wall. And David fled and escaped that night.

¹¹ Saul sent messengers to David's house to watch him, that he might kill him in the morning. But Michal, David's wife, told him, "If you do not escape with your life tonight, tomorrow you will be killed." ¹² So Michal let David down through the window, and he fled away and escaped. ¹³ Michal took an image and laid it on the bed and put a pillow of goats' hair at its head and covered it with the clothes. ¹⁴ And when Saul sent messengers to

take David, she said, "He is sick." ¹⁵ Then Saul sent the messengers to see David, saying, "Bring him up to me in the bed, that I may kill him." ¹⁶ And when the messengers came in, behold, the image was in the bed, with the pillow of goats' hair at its head. ¹⁷ Saul said to Michal, "Why have you deceived me thus and let my enemy go, so that he has escaped?" And Michal answered Saul, "He said to me, 'Let me go. Why should I kill you?'"

¹⁸ Now David fled and escaped, and he came to Samuel at Ramah and told him all that Saul had done to him. And he and Samuel went and lived at Naioth. ¹⁹ And it was told Saul, "Behold, David is at Naioth in Ramah." ²⁰ Then Saul sent messengers to take David, and when they saw the company of the prophets prophesying, and Samuel standing as head over them, the Spirit of God came upon the messengers of Saul, and they also prophesied. ²¹ When it was told Saul, he sent other messengers, and they also prophesied. And Saul sent messengers again the third time, and they also prophesied. ²² Then he himself went to Ramah and came to the great well that is in Secu. And he asked, "Where are Samuel and David?" And one said, "Behold, they are at Naioth in Ramah." ²³ And he went there to Naioth in Ramah. And the Spirit of God came upon him also, and as he went he prophesied until he came to Naioth in Ramah. ²⁴ And he too stripped off his clothes, and he too prophesied before Samuel and lay naked all that day and all that night. Thus it is said, "Is Saul also among the prophets?"

Jonathan Warns David

20 Then David fled from Naioth in Ramah and came and said before Jonathan, "What have I done? What is my guilt? And what is my sin before your father, that he seeks

my life?" ² And he said to him, "Far from it! You shall not die. Behold, my father does nothing either great or small without disclosing it to me. And why should my father hide this from me? It is not so." ³ But David vowed again, saying, "Your father knows well that I have found favor in your eyes, and he thinks, 'Do not let Jonathan know this, lest he be grieved.' But truly, as the LORD lives and as your soul lives, there is but a step between me and death." ⁴ Then Jonathan said to David, "Whatever you say, I will do for you." ⁵ David said to Jonathan, "Behold, tomorrow is the new moon, and I should not fail to sit at table with the king. But let me go, that I may hide myself in the field till the third day at evening. ⁶ If your father misses me at all, then say, 'David earnestly asked leave of me to run to Bethlehem his city, for there is a yearly sacrifice there for all the clan.' ⁷ If he says, 'Good!' it will be well with your servant, but if he is angry, then know that harm is determined by him. ⁸ Therefore deal kindly with your servant, for you have brought your servant into a covenant of the LORD with you. But if there is guilt in me, kill me yourself, for why should you bring me to your father?" ⁹ And Jonathan said, "Far be it from you! If I knew that it was determined by my father that harm should come to you, would I not tell you?" ¹⁰ Then David said to Jonathan, "Who will tell me if your father answers you roughly?" ¹¹ And Jonathan said to David, "Come, let us go out into the field." So they both went out into the field.

¹² And Jonathan said to David, "The LORD, the God of Israel, be witness! When I have sounded out my father, about this time tomorrow, or the third day, behold, if he is well disposed toward David, shall I not then send and disclose it to you? ¹³ But should it please my father to do you harm, the LORD do so to

Jonathan and more also if I do not disclose it to you and send you away, that you may go in safety. May the LORD be with you, as he has been with my father. ¹⁴ If I am still alive, show me the steadfast love of the LORD, that I may not die; ¹⁵ and do not cut off your steadfast love from my house forever, when the LORD cuts off every one of the enemies of David from the face of the earth." ¹⁶ And Jonathan made a covenant with the house of David, saying, "May the LORD take vengeance on David's enemies." ¹⁷ And Jonathan made David swear again by his love for him, for he loved him as he loved his own soul.

¹⁸ Then Jonathan said to him, "Tomorrow is the new moon, and you will be missed, because your seat will be empty. ¹⁹ On the third day go down quickly to the place where you hid yourself when the matter was in hand, and remain beside the stone heap. ²⁰ And I will shoot three arrows to the side of it, as though I shot at a mark. ²¹ And behold, I will send the boy, saying, 'Go, find the arrows.' If I say to the boy, 'Look, the arrows are on this side of you, take them,' then you are to come, for, as the LORD lives, it is safe for you and there is no danger. ²² But if I say to the youth, 'Look, the arrows are beyond you,' then go, for the LORD has sent you away. ²³ And as for the matter of which you and I have spoken, behold, the LORD is between you and me forever."

²⁴ So David hid himself in the field. And when the new moon came, the king sat down to eat food. ²⁵ The king sat on his seat, as at other times, on the seat by the wall. Jonathan sat opposite, and Abner sat by Saul's side, but David's place was empty.

²⁶ Yet Saul did not say anything that day, for he thought, "Something has happened to him. He is not clean; surely he is not clean." ²⁷ But on the second day, the day after the new moon, David's place was empty. And Saul said to Jonathan his

son, "Why has not the son of Jesse come to the meal, either yesterday or today?" ²⁸ Jonathan answered Saul, "David earnestly asked leave of me to go to Bethlehem. ²⁹ He said, 'Let me go, for our clan holds a sacrifice in the city, and my brother has commanded me to be there. So now, if I have found favor in your eyes, let me get away and see my brothers.' For this reason he has not come to the king's table."

³⁰ Then Saul's anger was kindled against Jonathan, and he said to him, "You son of a perverse, rebellious woman, do I not know that you have chosen the son of Jesse to your own shame, and to the shame of your mother's nakedness? ³¹ For as long as the son of Jesse lives on the earth, neither you nor your kingdom shall be established. Therefore send and bring him to me, for he shall surely die." ³² Then Jonathan answered Saul his father, "Why should he be put to death? What has he done?" ³³ But Saul hurled his spear at him to strike him. So Jonathan knew that his father was determined to put David to death. ³⁴ And Jonathan rose from the table in fierce anger and ate no food the second day of the month, for he was grieved for David, because his father had disgraced him.

³⁵ In the morning Jonathan went out into the field to the appointment with David, and with him a little boy. ³⁶ And he said to his boy, "Run and find the arrows that I shoot." As the boy ran, he shot an arrow beyond him. ³⁷ And when the boy came to the place of the arrow that Jonathan had shot, Jonathan called after the boy and said, "Is not the arrow beyond you?" ³⁸ And Jonathan called after the boy, "Hurry! Be quick! Do not stay!" So Jonathan's boy gathered up the arrows and came to his master. ³⁹ But the boy knew nothing. Only Jonathan and David knew the matter. ⁴⁰ And Jonathan gave his weapons to his boy

and said to him, "Go and carry them to the city." ⁴¹ And as soon as the boy had gone, David rose from beside the stone heap and fell on his face to the ground and bowed three times. And they kissed one another and wept with one another, David weeping the most. ⁴² Then Jonathan said to David, "Go in peace, because we have sworn both of us in the name of the LORD, saying, 'The LORD shall be between me and you, and between my offspring and your offspring, forever.'" And he rose and departed, and Jonathan went into the city.

David and the Holy Bread

21 Then David came to Nob, to Ahimelech the priest. And Ahimelech came to meet David, trembling, and said to him, "Why are you alone, and no one with you?" ² And David said to Ahimelech the priest, "The king has charged me with a matter and said to me, 'Let no one know anything of the matter about which I send you, and with which I have charged you.' I have made an appointment with the young men for such and such a place. ³ Now then, what do you have on hand? Give me five loaves of bread, or whatever is here." ⁴ And the priest answered David, "I have no common bread on hand, but there is holy bread—if the young men have kept themselves from women." ⁵ And David answered the priest, "Truly women have been kept from us as always when I go on an expedition. The vessels of the young men are holy even when it is an ordinary journey. How much more today will their vessels be holy?" ⁶ So the priest gave him the holy bread, for there was no bread there but the bread of the Presence, which is removed from before the LORD, to be replaced by hot bread on the day it is taken away.

⁷ Now a certain man of the servants of Saul was there that day, detained before the LORD. His name was Doeg the Edomite, the chief of Saul's herdsmen.

⁸ Then David said to Ahimelech, "Then have you not here a spear or a sword at hand? For I have brought neither my sword nor my weapons with me, because the king's business required haste." ⁹ And the priest said, "The sword of Goliath the Philistine, whom you struck down in the Valley of Elah, behold, it is here wrapped in a cloth behind the ephod. If you will take that, take it, for there is none but that here." And David said, "There is none like that; give it to me."

David Flees to Gath

¹⁰ And David rose and fled that day from Saul and went to Achish the king of Gath. ¹¹ And the servants of Achish said to him, "Is not this David the king of the land? Did they not sing to one another of him in dances,

'Saul has struck down his thousands,
      and David his ten thousands'?"

¹² And David took these words to heart and was much afraid of Achish the king of Gath. ¹³ So he changed his behavior before them and pretended to be insane in their hands and made marks on the doors of the gate and let his spittle run down his beard. ¹⁴ Then Achish said to his servants, "Behold, you see the man is mad. Why then have you brought him to me? ¹⁵ Do I lack madmen, that you have brought this fellow to behave as a madman in my presence? Shall this fellow come into my house?"

David at the Cave of Adullam

22 David departed from there and escaped to the cave of Adullam. And when his brothers and all his father's house heard it, they went down there to him. ²And everyone who was in distress, and everyone who was in debt, and everyone who was bitter in soul, gathered to him. And he became commander over them. And there were with him about four hundred men.

³And David went from there to Mizpeh of Moab. And he said to the king of Moab, "Please let my father and my mother stay with you, till I know what God will do for me." ⁴And he left them with the king of Moab, and they stayed with him all the time that David was in the stronghold. ⁵Then the prophet Gad said to David, "Do not remain in the stronghold; depart, and go into the land of Judah." So David departed and went into the forest of Hereth.

Saul Kills the Priests at Nob

⁶Now Saul heard that David was discovered, and the men who were with him. Saul was sitting at Gibeah under the tamarisk tree on the height with his spear in his hand, and all his servants were standing about him. ⁷And Saul said to his servants who stood about him, "Hear now, people of Benjamin; will the son of Jesse give every one of you fields and vineyards, will he make you all commanders of thousands and commanders of hundreds, ⁸that all of you have conspired against me? No one discloses to me when my son makes a covenant with the son of Jesse. None of you is sorry for me or discloses to me that my son has stirred up my servant against me, to lie in wait, as at this day." ⁹Then answered Doeg the Edomite, who stood by

the servants of Saul, "I saw the son of Jesse coming to Nob, to Ahimelech the son of Ahitub, ¹⁰ and he inquired of the LORD for him and gave him provisions and gave him the sword of Goliath the Philistine."

¹¹ Then the king sent to summon Ahimelech the priest, the son of Ahitub, and all his father's house, the priests who were at Nob, and all of them came to the king. ¹² And Saul said, "Hear now, son of Ahitub." And he answered, "Here I am, my lord." ¹³ And Saul said to him, "Why have you conspired against me, you and the son of Jesse, in that you have given him bread and a sword and have inquired of God for him, so that he has risen against me, to lie in wait, as at this day?" ¹⁴ Then Ahimelech answered the king, "And who among all your servants is so faithful as David, who is the king's son-in-law, and captain over your bodyguard, and honored in your house? ¹⁵ Is today the first time that I have inquired of God for him? No! Let not the king impute anything to his servant or to all the house of my father, for your servant has known nothing of all this, much or little." ¹⁶ And the king said, "You shall surely die, Ahimelech, you and all your father's house." ¹⁷ And the king said to the guard who stood about him, "Turn and kill the priests of the LORD, because their hand also is with David, and they knew that he fled and did not disclose it to me." But the servants of the king would not put out their hand to strike the priests of the LORD. ¹⁸ Then the king said to Doeg, "You turn and strike the priests." And Doeg the Edomite turned and struck down the priests, and he killed on that day eighty-five persons who wore the linen ephod. ¹⁹ And Nob, the city of the priests, he put to the sword; both man and woman, child and infant, ox, donkey and sheep, he put to the sword.

²⁰ But one of the sons of Ahimelech the son of Ahitub, named Abiathar, escaped and fled after David. ²¹ And Abiathar told David that Saul had killed the priests of the LORD. ²² And David said to Abiathar, "I knew on that day, when Doeg the Edomite was there, that he would surely tell Saul. I have occasioned the death of all the persons of your father's house. ²³ Stay with me; do not be afraid, for he who seeks my life seeks your life. With me you shall be in safekeeping."

David Saves the City of Keilah

23 Now they told David, "Behold, the Philistines are fighting against Keilah and are robbing the threshing floors." ² Therefore David inquired of the LORD, "Shall I go and attack these Philistines?" And the LORD said to David, "Go and attack the Philistines and save Keilah." ³ But David's men said to him, "Behold, we are afraid here in Judah; how much more then if we go to Keilah against the armies of the Philistines?" ⁴ Then David inquired of the LORD again. And the LORD answered him, "Arise, go down to Keilah, for I will give the Philistines into your hand." ⁵ And David and his men went to Keilah and fought with the Philistines and brought away their livestock and struck them with a great blow. So David saved the inhabitants of Keilah.

⁶ When Abiathar the son of Ahimelech had fled to David to Keilah, he had come down with an ephod in his hand. ⁷ Now it was told Saul that David had come to Keilah. And Saul said, "God has given him into my hand, for he has shut himself in by entering a town that has gates and bars." ⁸ And Saul summoned all the people to war, to go down to Keilah, to besiege David and his men. ⁹ David knew that Saul was plotting harm

against him. And he said to Abiathar the priest, "Bring the ephod here." ¹⁰ Then David said, "O LORD, the God of Israel, your servant has surely heard that Saul seeks to come to Keilah, to destroy the city on my account. ¹¹ Will the men of Keilah surrender me into his hand? Will Saul come down, as your servant has heard? O LORD, the God of Israel, please tell your servant." And the LORD said, "He will come down." ¹² Then David said, "Will the men of Keilah surrender me and my men into the hand of Saul?" And the LORD said, "They will surrender you." ¹³ Then David and his men, who were about six hundred, arose and departed from Keilah, and they went wherever they could go. When Saul was told that David had escaped from Keilah, he gave up the expedition. ¹⁴ And David remained in the strongholds in the wilderness, in the hill country of the wilderness of Ziph. And Saul sought him every day, but God did not give him into his hand.

Saul Pursues David

¹⁵ David saw that Saul had come out to seek his life. David was in the wilderness of Ziph at Horesh. ¹⁶ And Jonathan, Saul's son, rose and went to David at Horesh, and strengthened his hand in God. ¹⁷ And he said to him, "Do not fear, for the hand of Saul my father shall not find you. You shall be king over Israel, and I shall be next to you. Saul my father also knows this." ¹⁸ And the two of them made a covenant before the LORD. David remained at Horesh, and Jonathan went home.

¹⁹ Then the Ziphites went up to Saul at Gibeah, saying, "Is not David hiding among us in the strongholds at Horesh, on the hill of Hachilah, which is south of Jeshimon? ²⁰ Now come down, O king, according to all your heart's desire to come down,

and our part shall be to surrender him into the king's hand." ²¹ And Saul said, "May you be blessed by the LORD, for you have had compassion on me. ²² Go, make yet more sure. Know and see the place where his foot is, and who has seen him there, for it is told me that he is very cunning. ²³ See therefore and take note of all the lurking places where he hides, and come back to me with sure information. Then I will go with you. And if he is in the land, I will search him out among all the thousands of Judah." ²⁴ And they arose and went to Ziph ahead of Saul.

Now David and his men were in the wilderness of Maon, in the Arabah to the south of Jeshimon. ²⁵ And Saul and his men went to seek him. And David was told, so he went down to the rock and lived in the wilderness of Maon. And when Saul heard that, he pursued after David in the wilderness of Maon. ²⁶ Saul went on one side of the mountain, and David and his men on the other side of the mountain. And David was hurrying to get away from Saul. As Saul and his men were closing in on David and his men to capture them, ²⁷ a messenger came to Saul, saying, "Hurry and come, for the Philistines have made a raid against the land." ²⁸ So Saul returned from pursuing after David and went against the Philistines. Therefore that place was called the Rock of Escape. ²⁹ And David went up from there and lived in the strongholds of Engedi.

David Spares Saul's Life

24 When Saul returned from following the Philistines, he was told, "Behold, David is in the wilderness of Engedi." ² Then Saul took three thousand chosen men out of all Israel and went to seek David and his men in front of the Wildgoats' Rocks. ³ And he came to the sheepfolds by the way,

where there was a cave, and Saul went in to relieve himself. Now David and his men were sitting in the innermost parts of the cave. ⁴ And the men of David said to him, "Here is the day of which the LORD said to you, 'Behold, I will give your enemy into your hand, and you shall do to him as it shall seem good to you.'" Then David arose and stealthily cut off a corner of Saul's robe. ⁵ And afterward David's heart struck him, because he had cut off a corner of Saul's robe. ⁶ He said to his men, "The LORD forbid that I should do this thing to my lord, the LORD's anointed, to put out my hand against him, seeing he is the LORD's anointed." ⁷ So David persuaded his men with these words and did not permit them to attack Saul. And Saul rose up and left the cave and went on his way.

⁸ Afterward David also arose and went out of the cave, and called after Saul, "My lord the king!" And when Saul looked behind him, David bowed with his face to the earth and paid homage. ⁹ And David said to Saul, "Why do you listen to the words of men who say, 'Behold, David seeks your harm'? ¹⁰ Behold, this day your eyes have seen how the LORD gave you today into my hand in the cave. And some told me to kill you, but I spared you. I said, 'I will not put out my hand against my lord, for he is the LORD's anointed.' ¹¹ See, my father, see the corner of your robe in my hand. For by the fact that I cut off the corner of your robe and did not kill you, you may know and see that there is no wrong or treason in my hands. I have not sinned against you, though you hunt my life to take it. ¹² May the LORD judge between me and you, may the LORD avenge me against you, but my hand shall not be against you. ¹³ As the proverb of the ancients says, 'Out of the wicked comes wickedness.' But my hand shall not be against you. ¹⁴ After whom has

the king of Israel come out? After whom do you pursue? After a dead dog! After a flea! ¹⁵ May the LORD therefore be judge and give sentence between me and you, and see to it and plead my cause and deliver me from your hand."

¹⁶ As soon as David had finished speaking these words to Saul, Saul said, "Is this your voice, my son David?" And Saul lifted up his voice and wept. ¹⁷ He said to David, "You are more righteous than I, for you have repaid me good, whereas I have repaid you evil. ¹⁸ And you have declared this day how you have dealt well with me, in that you did not kill me when the LORD put me into your hands. ¹⁹ For if a man finds his enemy, will he let him go away safe? So may the LORD reward you with good for what you have done to me this day. ²⁰ And now, behold, I know that you shall surely be king, and that the kingdom of Israel shall be established in your hand. ²¹ Swear to me therefore by the LORD that you will not cut off my offspring after me, and that you will not destroy my name out of my father's house." ²² And David swore this to Saul. Then Saul went home, but David and his men went up to the stronghold.

The Death of Samuel

25 Now Samuel died. And all Israel assembled and mourned for him, and they buried him in his house at Ramah.

David and Abigail

Then David rose and went down to the wilderness of Paran. ² And there was a man in Maon whose business was in Carmel. The man was very rich; he had three thousand sheep and a thousand goats. He was shearing his sheep in Carmel.

³ Now the name of the man was Nabal, and the name of his wife Abigail. The woman was discerning and beautiful, but the man was harsh and badly behaved; he was a Calebite. ⁴ David heard in the wilderness that Nabal was shearing his sheep. ⁵ So David sent ten young men. And David said to the young men, "Go up to Carmel, and go to Nabal and greet him in my name. ⁶ And thus you shall greet him: 'Peace be to you, and peace be to your house, and peace be to all that you have. ⁷ I hear that you have shearers. Now your shepherds have been with us, and we did them no harm, and they missed nothing all the time they were in Carmel. ⁸ Ask your young men, and they will tell you. Therefore let my young men find favor in your eyes, for we come on a feast day. Please give whatever you have at hand to your servants and to your son David.' "

⁹ When David's young men came, they said all this to Nabal in the name of David, and then they waited. ¹⁰ And Nabal answered David's servants, "Who is David? Who is the son of Jesse? There are many servants these days who are breaking away from their masters. ¹¹ Shall I take my bread and my water and my meat that I have killed for my shearers and give it to men who come from I do not know where?" ¹² So David's young men turned away and came back and told him all this. ¹³ And David said to his men, "Every man strap on his sword!" And every man of them strapped on his sword. David also strapped on his sword. And about four hundred men went up after David, while two hundred remained with the baggage.

¹⁴ But one of the young men told Abigail, Nabal's wife, "Behold, David sent messengers out of the wilderness to greet our master, and he railed at them. ¹⁵ Yet the men were very good to us, and we suffered no harm, and we did not miss anything

when we were in the fields, as long as we went with them.
¹⁶ They were a wall to us both by night and by day, all the while
we were with them keeping the sheep. ¹⁷ Now therefore know
this and consider what you should do, for harm is determined
against our master and against all his house, and he is such a
worthless man that one cannot speak to him."

¹⁸ Then Abigail made haste and took two hundred loaves
and two skins of wine and five sheep already prepared and five
seahs of parched grain and a hundred clusters of raisins and
two hundred cakes of figs, and laid them on donkeys. ¹⁹ And
she said to her young men, "Go on before me; behold, I come
after you." But she did not tell her husband Nabal. ²⁰ And as
she rode on the donkey and came down under cover of the
mountain, behold, David and his men came down toward
her, and she met them. ²¹ Now David had said, "Surely in vain
have I guarded all that this fellow has in the wilderness, so that
nothing was missed of all that belonged to him, and he has
returned me evil for good. ²² God do so to the enemies of David
and more also, if by morning I leave so much as one male of all
who belong to him."

²³ When Abigail saw David, she hurried and got down from
the donkey and fell before David on her face and bowed to the
ground. ²⁴ She fell at his feet and said, "On me alone, my lord, be
the guilt. Please let your servant speak in your ears, and hear the
words of your servant. ²⁵ Let not my lord regard this worthless
fellow, Nabal, for as his name is, so is he. Nabal is his name, and
folly is with him. But I your servant did not see the young men
of my lord, whom you sent. ²⁶ Now then, my lord, as the LORD
lives, and as your soul lives, because the LORD has restrained
you from bloodguilt and from saving with your own hand,

now then let your enemies and those who seek to do evil to my lord be as Nabal. ²⁷ And now let this present that your servant has brought to my lord be given to the young men who follow my lord. ²⁸ Please forgive the trespass of your servant. For the LORD will certainly make my lord a sure house, because my lord is fighting the battles of the LORD, and evil shall not be found in you so long as you live. ²⁹ If men rise up to pursue you and to seek your life, the life of my lord shall be bound in the bundle of the living in the care of the LORD your God. And the lives of your enemies he shall sling out as from the hollow of a sling. ³⁰ And when the LORD has done to my lord according to all the good that he has spoken concerning you and has appointed you prince over Israel, ³¹ my lord shall have no cause of grief or pangs of conscience for having shed blood without cause or for my lord working salvation himself. And when the LORD has dealt well with my lord, then remember your servant."

³² And David said to Abigail, "Blessed be the LORD, the God of Israel, who sent you this day to meet me! ³³ Blessed be your discretion, and blessed be you, who have kept me this day from bloodguilt and from working salvation with my own hand! ³⁴ For as surely as the LORD, the God of Israel, lives, who has restrained me from hurting you, unless you had hurried and come to meet me, truly by morning there had not been left to Nabal so much as one male." ³⁵ Then David received from her hand what she had brought him. And he said to her, "Go up in peace to your house. See, I have obeyed your voice, and I have granted your petition."

³⁶ And Abigail came to Nabal, and behold, he was holding a feast in his house, like the feast of a king. And Nabal's heart was merry within him, for he was very drunk. So she told him

nothing at all until the morning light. ³⁷ In the morning, when the wine had gone out of Nabal, his wife told him these things, and his heart died within him, and he became as a stone. ³⁸ And about ten days later the LORD struck Nabal, and he died.

³⁹ When David heard that Nabal was dead, he said, "Blessed be the LORD who has avenged the insult I received at the hand of Nabal, and has kept back his servant from wrongdoing. The LORD has returned the evil of Nabal on his own head." Then David sent and spoke to Abigail, to take her as his wife. ⁴⁰ When the servants of David came to Abigail at Carmel, they said to her, "David has sent us to you to take you to him as his wife." ⁴¹ And she rose and bowed with her face to the ground and said, "Behold, your handmaid is a servant to wash the feet of the servants of my lord." ⁴² And Abigail hurried and rose and mounted a donkey, and her five young women attended her. She followed the messengers of David and became his wife.

⁴³ David also took Ahinoam of Jezreel, and both of them became his wives. ⁴⁴ Saul had given Michal his daughter, David's wife, to Palti the son of Laish, who was of Gallim.

David Spares Saul Again

26 Then the Ziphites came to Saul at Gibeah, saying, "Is not David hiding himself on the hill of Hachilah, which is on the east of Jeshimon?" ² So Saul arose and went down to the wilderness of Ziph with three thousand chosen men of Israel to seek David in the wilderness of Ziph. ³ And Saul encamped on the hill of Hachilah, which is beside the road on the east of Jeshimon. But David remained in the wilderness. When he saw that Saul came after him into the wilderness, ⁴ David sent out spies and learned that Saul had indeed

come. ⁵ Then David rose and came to the place where Saul had encamped. And David saw the place where Saul lay, with Abner the son of Ner, the commander of his army. Saul was lying within the encampment, while the army was encamped around him.

⁶ Then David said to Ahimelech the Hittite, and to Joab's brother Abishai the son of Zeruiah, "Who will go down with me into the camp to Saul?" And Abishai said, "I will go down with you." ⁷ So David and Abishai went to the army by night. And there lay Saul sleeping within the encampment, with his spear stuck in the ground at his head, and Abner and the army lay around him. ⁸ Then Abishai said to David, "God has given your enemy into your hand this day. Now please let me pin him to the earth with one stroke of the spear, and I will not strike him twice." ⁹ But David said to Abishai, "Do not destroy him, for who can put out his hand against the LORD's anointed and be guiltless?" ¹⁰ And David said, "As the LORD lives, the LORD will strike him, or his day will come to die, or he will go down into battle and perish. ¹¹ The LORD forbid that I should put out my hand against the LORD's anointed. But take now the spear that is at his head and the jar of water, and let us go." ¹² So David took the spear and the jar of water from Saul's head, and they went away. No man saw it or knew it, nor did any awake, for they were all asleep, because a deep sleep from the LORD had fallen upon them.

¹³ Then David went over to the other side and stood far off on the top of the hill, with a great space between them. ¹⁴ And David called to the army, and to Abner the son of Ner, saying, "Will you not answer, Abner?" Then Abner answered, "Who are you who calls to the king?" ¹⁵ And David said to Abner, "Are you

not a man? Who is like you in Israel? Why then have you not kept watch over your lord the king? For one of the people came in to destroy the king your lord. ¹⁶ This thing that you have done is not good. As the LORD lives, you deserve to die, because you have not kept watch over your lord, the LORD's anointed. And now see where the king's spear is and the jar of water that was at his head."

¹⁷ Saul recognized David's voice and said, "Is this your voice, my son David?" And David said, "It is my voice, my lord, O king." ¹⁸ And he said, "Why does my lord pursue after his servant? For what have I done? What evil is on my hands? ¹⁹ Now therefore let my lord the king hear the words of his servant. If it is the LORD who has stirred you up against me, may he accept an offering, but if it is men, may they be cursed before the LORD, for they have driven me out this day that I should have no share in the heritage of the LORD, saying, 'Go, serve other gods.' ²⁰ Now therefore, let not my blood fall to the earth away from the presence of the LORD, for the king of Israel has come out to seek a single flea like one who hunts a partridge in the mountains."

²¹ Then Saul said, "I have sinned. Return, my son David, for I will no more do you harm, because my life was precious in your eyes this day. Behold, I have acted foolishly, and have made a great mistake." ²² And David answered and said, "Here is the spear, O king! Let one of the young men come over and take it. ²³ The LORD rewards every man for his righteousness and his faithfulness, for the LORD gave you into my hand today, and I would not put out my hand against the LORD's anointed. ²⁴ Behold, as your life was precious this day in my sight, so may my life be precious in the sight of the LORD, and may he deliver me out of all tribulation." ²⁵ Then Saul said to David, "Blessed

be you, my son David! You will do many things and will succeed in them." So David went his way, and Saul returned to his place.

David Flees to the Philistines

27 Then David said in his heart, "Now I shall perish one day by the hand of Saul. There is nothing better for me than that I should escape to the land of the Philistines. Then Saul will despair of seeking me any longer within the borders of Israel, and I shall escape out of his hand." ² So David arose and went over, he and the six hundred men who were with him, to Achish the son of Maoch, king of Gath. ³ And David lived with Achish at Gath, he and his men, every man with his household, and David with his two wives, Ahinoam of Jezreel, and Abigail of Carmel, Nabal's widow. ⁴ And when it was told Saul that David had fled to Gath, he no longer sought him.

⁵ Then David said to Achish, "If I have found favor in your eyes, let a place be given me in one of the country towns, that I may dwell there. For why should your servant dwell in the royal city with you?" ⁶ So that day Achish gave him Ziklag. Therefore Ziklag has belonged to the kings of Judah to this day. ⁷ And the number of the days that David lived in the country of the Philistines was a year and four months.

⁸ Now David and his men went up and made raids against the Geshurites, the Girzites, and the Amalekites, for these were the inhabitants of the land from of old, as far as Shur, to the land of Egypt. ⁹ And David would strike the land and would leave neither man nor woman alive, but would take away the sheep, the oxen, the donkeys, the camels, and the garments, and come back to Achish. ¹⁰ When Achish asked, "Where have you made a raid today?" David would say, "Against the Negeb

of Judah," or, "Against the Negeb of the Jerahmeelites," or, "Against the Negeb of the Kenites." ¹¹ And David would leave neither man nor woman alive to bring news to Gath, thinking, "lest they should tell about us and say, 'So David has done.'" Such was his custom all the while he lived in the country of the Philistines. ¹² And Achish trusted David, thinking, "He has made himself an utter stench to his people Israel; therefore he shall always be my servant."

Saul and the Medium of En-dor

28 In those days the Philistines gathered their forces for war, to fight against Israel. And Achish said to David, "Understand that you and your men are to go out with me in the army." ² David said to Achish, "Very well, you shall know what your servant can do." And Achish said to David, "Very well, I will make you my bodyguard for life."

³ Now Samuel had died, and all Israel had mourned for him and buried him in Ramah, his own city. And Saul had put the mediums and the necromancers out of the land. ⁴ The Philistines assembled and came and encamped at Shunem. And Saul gathered all Israel, and they encamped at Gilboa. ⁵ When Saul saw the army of the Philistines, he was afraid, and his heart trembled greatly. ⁶ And when Saul inquired of the LORD, the LORD did not answer him, either by dreams, or by Urim, or by prophets. ⁷ Then Saul said to his servants, "Seek out for me a woman who is a medium, that I may go to her and inquire of her." And his servants said to him, "Behold, there is a medium at En-dor."

⁸ So Saul disguised himself and put on other garments and went, he and two men with him. And they came to the woman by night. And he said, "Divine for me by a spirit and bring up

for me whomever I shall name to you." **9** The woman said to him, "Surely you know what Saul has done, how he has cut off the mediums and the necromancers from the land. Why then are you laying a trap for my life to bring about my death?" **10** But Saul swore to her by the LORD, "As the LORD lives, no punishment shall come upon you for this thing." **11** Then the woman said, "Whom shall I bring up for you?" He said, "Bring up Samuel for me." **12** When the woman saw Samuel, she cried out with a loud voice. And the woman said to Saul, "Why have you deceived me? You are Saul." **13** The king said to her, "Do not be afraid. What do you see?" And the woman said to Saul, "I see a god coming up out of the earth." **14** He said to her, "What is his appearance?" And she said, "An old man is coming up, and he is wrapped in a robe." And Saul knew that it was Samuel, and he bowed with his face to the ground and paid homage.

15 Then Samuel said to Saul, "Why have you disturbed me by bringing me up?" Saul answered, "I am in great distress, for the Philistines are warring against me, and God has turned away from me and answers me no more, either by prophets or by dreams. Therefore I have summoned you to tell me what I shall do." **16** And Samuel said, "Why then do you ask me, since the LORD has turned from you and become your enemy? **17** The LORD has done to you as he spoke by me, for the LORD has torn the kingdom out of your hand and given it to your neighbor, David. **18** Because you did not obey the voice of the LORD and did not carry out his fierce wrath against Amalek, therefore the LORD has done this thing to you this day. **19** Moreover, the LORD will give Israel also with you into the hand of the Philistines, and tomorrow you and your sons shall be with me. The LORD will give the army of Israel also into the hand of the Philistines."

²⁰ Then Saul fell at once full length on the ground, filled with fear because of the words of Samuel. And there was no strength in him, for he had eaten nothing all day and all night. ²¹ And the woman came to Saul, and when she saw that he was terrified, she said to him, "Behold, your servant has obeyed you. I have taken my life in my hand and have listened to what you have said to me. ²² Now therefore, you also obey your servant. Let me set a morsel of bread before you; and eat, that you may have strength when you go on your way." ²³ He refused and said, "I will not eat." But his servants, together with the woman, urged him, and he listened to their words. So he arose from the earth and sat on the bed. ²⁴ Now the woman had a fattened calf in the house, and she quickly killed it, and she took flour and kneaded it and baked unleavened bread of it, ²⁵ and she put it before Saul and his servants, and they ate. Then they rose and went away that night.

The Philistines Reject David

29 Now the Philistines had gathered all their forces at Aphek. And the Israelites were encamped by the spring that is in Jezreel. ² As the lords of the Philistines were passing on by hundreds and by thousands, and David and his men were passing on in the rear with Achish, ³ the commanders of the Philistines said, "What are these Hebrews doing here?" And Achish said to the commanders of the Philistines, "Is this not David, the servant of Saul, king of Israel, who has been with me now for days and years, and since he deserted to me I have found no fault in him to this day." ⁴ But the commanders of the Philistines were angry with him. And the commanders of the Philistines said to him, "Send the man back, that he may return to the place to which you have assigned him. He shall

not go down with us to battle, lest in the battle he become an adversary to us. For how could this fellow reconcile himself to his lord? Would it not be with the heads of the men here? ⁵ Is not this David, of whom they sing to one another in dances,

> 'Saul has struck down his thousands,
>   and David his ten thousands'?"

⁶ Then Achish called David and said to him, "As the LORD lives, you have been honest, and to me it seems right that you should march out and in with me in the campaign. For I have found nothing wrong in you from the day of your coming to me to this day. Nevertheless, the lords do not approve of you. ⁷ So go back now; and go peaceably, that you may not displease the lords of the Philistines." ⁸ And David said to Achish, "But what have I done? What have you found in your servant from the day I entered your service until now, that I may not go and fight against the enemies of my lord the king?" ⁹ And Achish answered David and said, "I know that you are as blameless in my sight as an angel of God. Nevertheless, the commanders of the Philistines have said, 'He shall not go up with us to the battle.' ¹⁰ Now then rise early in the morning with the servants of your lord who came with you, and start early in the morning, and depart as soon as you have light." ¹¹ So David set out with his men early in the morning to return to the land of the Philistines. But the Philistines went up to Jezreel.

David's Wives Are Captured

30 Now when David and his men came to Ziklag on the third day, the Amalekites had made a raid against the Negeb and against Ziklag. They had overcome Ziklag and

burned it with fire ²and taken captive the women and all who were in it, both small and great. They killed no one, but carried them off and went their way. ³And when David and his men came to the city, they found it burned with fire, and their wives and sons and daughters taken captive. ⁴Then David and the people who were with him raised their voices and wept until they had no more strength to weep. ⁵David's two wives also had been taken captive, Ahinoam of Jezreel and Abigail the widow of Nabal of Carmel. ⁶And David was greatly distressed, for the people spoke of stoning him, because all the people were bitter in soul, each for his sons and daughters. But David strengthened himself in the LORD his God.

⁷And David said to Abiathar the priest, the son of Ahimelech, "Bring me the ephod." So Abiathar brought the ephod to David. ⁸And David inquired of the LORD, "Shall I pursue after this band? Shall I overtake them?" He answered him, "Pursue, for you shall surely overtake and shall surely rescue." ⁹So David set out, and the six hundred men who were with him, and they came to the brook Besor, where those who were left behind stayed. ¹⁰But David pursued, he and four hundred men. Two hundred stayed behind, who were too exhausted to cross the brook Besor.

¹¹They found an Egyptian in the open country and brought him to David. And they gave him bread and he ate. They gave him water to drink, ¹²and they gave him a piece of a cake of figs and two clusters of raisins. And when he had eaten, his spirit revived, for he had not eaten bread or drunk water for three days and three nights. ¹³And David said to him, "To whom do you belong? And where are you from?" He said, "I am a young man of Egypt, servant to an Amalekite, and my master left me

behind because I fell sick three days ago. ¹⁴ We had made a raid against the Negeb of the Cherethites and against that which belongs to Judah and against the Negeb of Caleb, and we burned Ziklag with fire." ¹⁵ And David said to him, "Will you take me down to this band?" And he said, "Swear to me by God that you will not kill me or deliver me into the hands of my master, and I will take you down to this band."

David Defeats the Amalekites

¹⁶ And when he had taken him down, behold, they were spread abroad over all the land, eating and drinking and dancing, because of all the great spoil they had taken from the land of the Philistines and from the land of Judah. ¹⁷ And David struck them down from twilight until the evening of the next day, and not a man of them escaped, except four hundred young men, who mounted camels and fled. ¹⁸ David recovered all that the Amalekites had taken, and David rescued his two wives. ¹⁹ Nothing was missing, whether small or great, sons or daughters, spoil or anything that had been taken. David brought back all. ²⁰ David also captured all the flocks and herds, and the people drove the livestock before him, and said, "This is David's spoil."

²¹ Then David came to the two hundred men who had been too exhausted to follow David, and who had been left at the brook Besor. And they went out to meet David and to meet the people who were with him. And when David came near to the people he greeted them. ²² Then all the wicked and worthless fellows among the men who had gone with David said, "Because they did not go with us, we will not give them any of the spoil that we have recovered, except that each man may lead

away his wife and children, and depart." ²³ But David said, "You shall not do so, my brothers, with what the LORD has given us. He has preserved us and given into our hand the band that came against us. ²⁴ Who would listen to you in this matter? For as his share is who goes down into the battle, so shall his share be who stays by the baggage. They shall share alike." ²⁵ And he made it a statute and a rule for Israel from that day forward to this day.

²⁶ When David came to Ziklag, he sent part of the spoil to his friends, the elders of Judah, saying, "Here is a present for you from the spoil of the enemies of the LORD." ²⁷ It was for those in Bethel, in Ramoth of the Negeb, in Jattir, ²⁸ in Aroer, in Siphmoth, in Eshtemoa, ²⁹ in Racal, in the cities of the Jerahmeelites, in the cities of the Kenites, ³⁰ in Hormah, in Borashan, in Athach, ³¹ in Hebron, for all the places where David and his men had roamed.

The Death of Saul

31 Now the Philistines were fighting against Israel, and the men of Israel fled before the Philistines and fell slain on Mount Gilboa. ² And the Philistines overtook Saul and his sons, and the Philistines struck down Jonathan and Abinadab and Malchi-shua, the sons of Saul. ³ The battle pressed hard against Saul, and the archers found him, and he was badly wounded by the archers. ⁴ Then Saul said to his armor-bearer, "Draw your sword, and thrust me through with it, lest these uncircumcised come and thrust me through, and mistreat me." But his armor-bearer would not, for he feared greatly. Therefore Saul took his own sword and fell upon it. ⁵ And when his armor-bearer saw that Saul was dead, he also fell upon his sword and died with

him. ⁶ Thus Saul died, and his three sons, and his armor-bearer, and all his men, on the same day together. ⁷ And when the men of Israel who were on the other side of the valley and those beyond the Jordan saw that the men of Israel had fled and that Saul and his sons were dead, they abandoned their cities and fled. And the Philistines came and lived in them.

⁸ The next day, when the Philistines came to strip the slain, they found Saul and his three sons fallen on Mount Gilboa. ⁹ So they cut off his head and stripped off his armor and sent messengers throughout the land of the Philistines, to carry the good news to the house of their idols and to the people. ¹⁰ They put his armor in the temple of Ashtaroth, and they fastened his body to the wall of Beth-shan. ¹¹ But when the inhabitants of Jabesh-gilead heard what the Philistines had done to Saul, ¹² all the valiant men arose and went all night and took the body of Saul and the bodies of his sons from the wall of Beth-shan, and they came to Jabesh and burned them there. ¹³ And they took their bones and buried them under the tamarisk tree in Jabesh and fasted seven days.

2 SAMUEL

David Hears of Saul's Death

1 After the death of Saul, when David had returned from striking down the Amalekites, David remained two days in Ziklag. ² And on the third day, behold, a man came from Saul's camp, with his clothes torn and dirt on his head. And when he came to David, he fell to the ground and paid homage. ³ David said to him, "Where do you come from?" And he said to him, "I have escaped from the camp of Israel." ⁴ And David said to him, "How did it go? Tell me." And he answered, "The people fled from the battle, and also many of the people have fallen and are dead, and Saul and his son Jonathan are also dead." ⁵ Then David said to the young man who told him, "How do you know that Saul and his son Jonathan are dead?" ⁶ And the young man who told him said, "By chance I happened to be on Mount Gilboa, and there was Saul leaning on his spear, and behold, the chariots and the horsemen were close upon him. ⁷ And when he looked behind him, he saw me, and called to me. And I answered, 'Here I am.' ⁸ And he said to me, 'Who are you?' I answered him, 'I am an Amalekite.' ⁹ And he said to me, 'Stand beside me and kill me, for anguish has seized me, and yet my life still lingers.' ¹⁰ So I stood beside him and killed him, because I was sure that he could not live after he had fallen. And I took the crown that was on his head and the armlet that was on his arm, and I have brought them here to my lord."

¹¹ Then David took hold of his clothes and tore them, and so did all the men who were with him. ¹² And they mourned and wept and fasted until evening for Saul and for Jonathan his son and for the people of the LORD and for the house of Israel, because they had fallen by the sword. ¹³ And David said to the young man who told him, "Where do you come from?" And he answered, "I am the son of a sojourner, an Amalekite." ¹⁴ David said to him, "How is it you were not afraid to put out your hand to destroy the LORD's anointed?" ¹⁵ Then David called one of the young men and said, "Go, execute him." And he struck him down so that he died. ¹⁶ And David said to him, "Your blood be on your head, for your own mouth has testified against you, saying, 'I have killed the LORD's anointed.'"

David's Lament for Saul and Jonathan

¹⁷ And David lamented with this lamentation over Saul and Jonathan his son, ¹⁸ and he said it should be taught to the people of Judah; behold, it is written in the Book of Jashar. He said:

¹⁹   "Your glory, O Israel, is slain on your high places!
            How the mighty have fallen!
²⁰   Tell it not in Gath,
            publish it not in the streets of Ashkelon,
        lest the daughters of the Philistines rejoice,
            lest the daughters of the uncircumcised exult.

²¹   "You mountains of Gilboa,
            let there be no dew or rain upon you,
            nor fields of offerings!

For there the shield of the mighty was defiled,
    the shield of Saul, not anointed with oil.

22 "From the blood of the slain,
    from the fat of the mighty,
the bow of Jonathan turned not back,
    and the sword of Saul returned not empty.

23 "Saul and Jonathan, beloved and lovely!
    In life and in death they were not divided;
they were swifter than eagles;
    they were stronger than lions.

24 "You daughters of Israel, weep over Saul,
    who clothed you luxuriously in scarlet,
    who put ornaments of gold on your
        apparel.

25 "How the mighty have fallen
    in the midst of the battle!

"Jonathan lies slain on your high places.
26   I am distressed for you, my brother
      Jonathan;
very pleasant have you been to me;
    your love to me was extraordinary,
    surpassing the love of women.

27 "How the mighty have fallen,
    and the weapons of war perished!"

David Anointed King of Judah

2 After this David inquired of the LORD, "Shall I go up into any of the cities of Judah?" And the LORD said to him, "Go up." David said, "To which shall I go up?" And he said, "To Hebron." **²** So David went up there, and his two wives also, Ahinoam of Jezreel and Abigail the widow of Nabal of Carmel. **³** And David brought up his men who were with him, everyone with his household, and they lived in the towns of Hebron. **⁴** And the men of Judah came, and there they anointed David king over the house of Judah.

When they told David, "It was the men of Jabesh-gilead who buried Saul," **⁵** David sent messengers to the men of Jabesh-gilead and said to them, "May you be blessed by the LORD, because you showed this loyalty to Saul your lord and buried him. **⁶** Now may the LORD show steadfast love and faithfulness to you. And I will do good to you because you have done this thing. **⁷** Now therefore let your hands be strong, and be valiant, for Saul your lord is dead, and the house of Judah has anointed me king over them."

Ish-bosheth Made King of Israel

⁸ But Abner the son of Ner, commander of Saul's army, took Ish-bosheth the son of Saul and brought him over to Mahanaim, **⁹** and he made him king over Gilead and the Ashurites and Jezreel and Ephraim and Benjamin and all Israel. **¹⁰** Ish-bosheth, Saul's son, was forty years old when he began to reign over Israel, and he reigned two years. But the house of Judah followed David. **¹¹** And the time that David was king in Hebron over the house of Judah was seven years and six months.

The Battle of Gibeon

¹²Abner the son of Ner, and the servants of Ish-bosheth the son of Saul, went out from Mahanaim to Gibeon. ¹³And Joab the son of Zeruiah and the servants of David went out and met them at the pool of Gibeon. And they sat down, the one on the one side of the pool, and the other on the other side of the pool. ¹⁴And Abner said to Joab, "Let the young men arise and compete before us." And Joab said, "Let them arise." ¹⁵Then they arose and passed over by number, twelve for Benjamin and Ish-bosheth the son of Saul, and twelve of the servants of David. ¹⁶And each caught his opponent by the head and thrust his sword in his opponent's side, so they fell down together. Therefore that place was called Helkath-hazzurim, which is at Gibeon. ¹⁷And the battle was very fierce that day. And Abner and the men of Israel were beaten before the servants of David.

¹⁸And the three sons of Zeruiah were there, Joab, Abishai, and Asahel. Now Asahel was as swift of foot as a wild gazelle. ¹⁹And Asahel pursued Abner, and as he went, he turned neither to the right hand nor to the left from following Abner. ²⁰Then Abner looked behind him and said, "Is it you, Asahel?" And he answered, "It is I." ²¹Abner said to him, "Turn aside to your right hand or to your left, and seize one of the young men and take his spoil." But Asahel would not turn aside from following him. ²²And Abner said again to Asahel, "Turn aside from following me. Why should I strike you to the ground? How then could I lift up my face to your brother Joab?" ²³But he refused to turn aside. Therefore Abner struck him in the stomach with the butt of his spear, so that the spear came out at his back. And he fell there and died where he was. And all who came to the place where Asahel had fallen and died, stood still.

²⁴ But Joab and Abishai pursued Abner. And as the sun was going down they came to the hill of Ammah, which lies before Giah on the way to the wilderness of Gibeon. ²⁵ And the people of Benjamin gathered themselves together behind Abner and became one group and took their stand on the top of a hill. ²⁶ Then Abner called to Joab, "Shall the sword devour forever? Do you not know that the end will be bitter? How long will it be before you tell your people to turn from the pursuit of their brothers?" ²⁷ And Joab said, "As God lives, if you had not spoken, surely the men would not have given up the pursuit of their brothers until the morning." ²⁸ So Joab blew the trumpet, and all the men stopped and pursued Israel no more, nor did they fight anymore.

²⁹ And Abner and his men went all that night through the Arabah. They crossed the Jordan, and marching the whole morning, they came to Mahanaim. ³⁰ Joab returned from the pursuit of Abner. And when he had gathered all the people together, there were missing from David's servants nineteen men besides Asahel. ³¹ But the servants of David had struck down of Benjamin 360 of Abner's men. ³² And they took up Asahel and buried him in the tomb of his father, which was at Bethlehem. And Joab and his men marched all night, and the day broke upon them at Hebron.

Abner Joins David

3 There was a long war between the house of Saul and the house of David. And David grew stronger and stronger, while the house of Saul became weaker and weaker.

² And sons were born to David at Hebron: his firstborn was Amnon, of Ahinoam of Jezreel; ³ and his second, Chileab, of

Abigail the widow of Nabal of Carmel; and the third, Absalom the son of Maacah the daughter of Talmai king of Geshur; **⁴** and the fourth, Adonijah the son of Haggith; and the fifth, Shephatiah the son of Abital; **⁵** and the sixth, Ithream, of Eglah, David's wife. These were born to David in Hebron.

⁶ While there was war between the house of Saul and the house of David, Abner was making himself strong in the house of Saul. **⁷** Now Saul had a concubine whose name was Rizpah, the daughter of Aiah. And Ish-bosheth said to Abner, "Why have you gone in to my father's concubine?" **⁸** Then Abner was very angry over the words of Ish-bosheth and said, "Am I a dog's head of Judah? To this day I keep showing steadfast love to the house of Saul your father, to his brothers, and to his friends, and have not given you into the hand of David. And yet you charge me today with a fault concerning a woman. **⁹** God do so to Abner and more also, if I do not accomplish for David what the LORD has sworn to him, **¹⁰** to transfer the kingdom from the house of Saul and set up the throne of David over Israel and over Judah, from Dan to Beersheba." **¹¹** And Ish-bosheth could not answer Abner another word, because he feared him.

¹² And Abner sent messengers to David on his behalf, saying, "To whom does the land belong? Make your covenant with me, and behold, my hand shall be with you to bring over all Israel to you." **¹³** And he said, "Good; I will make a covenant with you. But one thing I require of you; that is, you shall not see my face unless you first bring Michal, Saul's daughter, when you come to see my face." **¹⁴** Then David sent messengers to Ish-bosheth, Saul's son, saying, "Give me my wife Michal, for whom I paid the bridal price of a hundred foreskins of the Philistines."

¹⁵ And Ish-bosheth sent and took her from her husband Paltiel the son of Laish. ¹⁶ But her husband went with her, weeping after her all the way to Bahurim. Then Abner said to him, "Go, return." And he returned.

¹⁷ And Abner conferred with the elders of Israel, saying, "For some time past you have been seeking David as king over you. ¹⁸ Now then bring it about, for the LORD has promised David, saying, 'By the hand of my servant David I will save my people Israel from the hand of the Philistines, and from the hand of all their enemies.'" ¹⁹ Abner also spoke to Benjamin. And then Abner went to tell David at Hebron all that Israel and the whole house of Benjamin thought good to do.

²⁰ When Abner came with twenty men to David at Hebron, David made a feast for Abner and the men who were with him. ²¹ And Abner said to David, "I will arise and go and will gather all Israel to my lord the king, that they may make a covenant with you, and that you may reign over all that your heart desires." So David sent Abner away, and he went in peace.

²² Just then the servants of David arrived with Joab from a raid, bringing much spoil with them. But Abner was not with David at Hebron, for he had sent him away, and he had gone in peace. ²³ When Joab and all the army that was with him came, it was told Joab, "Abner the son of Ner came to the king, and he has let him go, and he has gone in peace." ²⁴ Then Joab went to the king and said, "What have you done? Behold, Abner came to you. Why is it that you have sent him away, so that he is gone? ²⁵ You know that Abner the son of Ner came to deceive you and to know your going out and your coming in, and to know all that you are doing."

Joab Murders Abner

²⁶ When Joab came out from David's presence, he sent messengers after Abner, and they brought him back from the cistern of Sirah. But David did not know about it. ²⁷ And when Abner returned to Hebron, Joab took him aside into the midst of the gate to speak with him privately, and there he struck him in the stomach, so that he died, for the blood of Asahel his brother. ²⁸ Afterward, when David heard of it, he said, "I and my kingdom are forever guiltless before the Lord for the blood of Abner the son of Ner. ²⁹ May it fall upon the head of Joab and upon all his father's house, and may the house of Joab never be without one who has a discharge or who is leprous or who holds a spindle or who falls by the sword or who lacks bread!" ³⁰ So Joab and Abishai his brother killed Abner, because he had put their brother Asahel to death in the battle at Gibeon.

David Mourns Abner

³¹ Then David said to Joab and to all the people who were with him, "Tear your clothes and put on sackcloth and mourn before Abner." And King David followed the bier. ³² They buried Abner at Hebron. And the king lifted up his voice and wept at the grave of Abner, and all the people wept. ³³ And the king lamented for Abner, saying,

> "Should Abner die as a fool dies?
> ³⁴   Your hands were not bound;
> > your feet were not fettered;
> as one falls before the wicked
> > you have fallen."

And all the people wept again over him. ³⁵ Then all the people came to persuade David to eat bread while it was yet day. But David swore, saying, "God do so to me and more also, if I taste bread or anything else till the sun goes down!" ³⁶ And all the people took notice of it, and it pleased them, as everything that the king did pleased all the people. ³⁷ So all the people and all Israel understood that day that it had not been the king's will to put to death Abner the son of Ner. ³⁸ And the king said to his servants, "Do you not know that a prince and a great man has fallen this day in Israel? ³⁹ And I was gentle today, though anointed king. These men, the sons of Zeruiah, are more severe than I. The LORD repay the evildoer according to his wickedness!"

Ish-bosheth Murdered

4 When Ish-bosheth, Saul's son, heard that Abner had died at Hebron, his courage failed, and all Israel was dismayed. ² Now Saul's son had two men who were captains of raiding bands; the name of the one was Baanah, and the name of the other Rechab, sons of Rimmon a man of Benjamin from Beeroth (for Beeroth also is counted part of Benjamin; ³ the Beerothites fled to Gittaim and have been sojourners there to this day).

⁴ Jonathan, the son of Saul, had a son who was crippled in his feet. He was five years old when the news about Saul and Jonathan came from Jezreel, and his nurse took him up and fled, and as she fled in her haste, he fell and became lame. And his name was Mephibosheth.

⁵ Now the sons of Rimmon the Beerothite, Rechab and Baanah, set out, and about the heat of the day they came to the house of Ish-bosheth as he was taking his noonday rest. ⁶ And

they came into the midst of the house as if to get wheat, and they stabbed him in the stomach. Then Rechab and Baanah his brother escaped. ⁷When they came into the house, as he lay on his bed in his bedroom, they struck him and put him to death and beheaded him. They took his head and went by the way of the Arabah all night, ⁸and brought the head of Ish-bosheth to David at Hebron. And they said to the king, "Here is the head of Ish-bosheth, the son of Saul, your enemy, who sought your life. The LORD has avenged my lord the king this day on Saul and on his offspring." ⁹But David answered Rechab and Baanah his brother, the sons of Rimmon the Beerothite, "As the LORD lives, who has redeemed my life out of every adversity, ¹⁰when one told me, 'Behold, Saul is dead,' and thought he was bringing good news, I seized him and killed him at Ziklag, which was the reward I gave him for his news. ¹¹How much more, when wicked men have killed a righteous man in his own house on his bed, shall I not now require his blood at your hand and destroy you from the earth?" ¹²And David commanded his young men, and they killed them and cut off their hands and feet and hanged them beside the pool at Hebron. But they took the head of Ish-bosheth and buried it in the tomb of Abner at Hebron.

David Anointed King of Israel

5 Then all the tribes of Israel came to David at Hebron and said, "Behold, we are your bone and flesh. ²In times past, when Saul was king over us, it was you who led out and brought in Israel. And the LORD said to you, 'You shall be shepherd of my people Israel, and you shall be prince over Israel.'" ³So all the elders of Israel came to the king at Hebron, and

King David made a covenant with them at Hebron before the LORD, and they anointed David king over Israel. ⁴David was thirty years old when he began to reign, and he reigned forty years. ⁵At Hebron he reigned over Judah seven years and six months, and at Jerusalem he reigned over all Israel and Judah thirty-three years.

⁶And the king and his men went to Jerusalem against the Jebusites, the inhabitants of the land, who said to David, "You will not come in here, but the blind and the lame will ward you off"—thinking, "David cannot come in here." ⁷Nevertheless, David took the stronghold of Zion, that is, the city of David. ⁸And David said on that day, "Whoever would strike the Jebusites, let him get up the water shaft to attack 'the lame and the blind,' who are hated by David's soul." Therefore it is said, "The blind and the lame shall not come into the house." ⁹And David lived in the stronghold and called it the city of David. And David built the city all around from the Millo inward. ¹⁰And David became greater and greater, for the LORD, the God of hosts, was with him.

¹¹And Hiram king of Tyre sent messengers to David, and cedar trees, also carpenters and masons who built David a house. ¹²And David knew that the LORD had established him king over Israel, and that he had exalted his kingdom for the sake of his people Israel.

¹³And David took more concubines and wives from Jerusalem, after he came from Hebron, and more sons and daughters were born to David. ¹⁴And these are the names of those who were born to him in Jerusalem: Shammua, Shobab, Nathan, Solomon, ¹⁵Ibhar, Elishua, Nepheg, Japhia, ¹⁶Elishama, Eliada, and Eliphelet.

David Defeats the Philistines

¹⁷ When the Philistines heard that David had been anointed king over Israel, all the Philistines went up to search for David. But David heard of it and went down to the stronghold. ¹⁸ Now the Philistines had come and spread out in the Valley of Rephaim. ¹⁹ And David inquired of the LORD, "Shall I go up against the Philistines? Will you give them into my hand?" And the LORD said to David, "Go up, for I will certainly give the Philistines into your hand." ²⁰ And David came to Baal-perazim, and David defeated them there. And he said, "The LORD has broken through my enemies before me like a breaking flood." Therefore the name of that place is called Baal-perazim. ²¹ And the Philistines left their idols there, and David and his men carried them away.

²² And the Philistines came up yet again and spread out in the Valley of Rephaim. ²³ And when David inquired of the LORD, he said, "You shall not go up; go around to their rear, and come against them opposite the balsam trees. ²⁴ And when you hear the sound of marching in the tops of the balsam trees, then rouse yourself, for then the LORD has gone out before you to strike down the army of the Philistines." ²⁵ And David did as the LORD commanded him, and struck down the Philistines from Geba to Gezer.

The Ark Brought to Jerusalem

6 David again gathered all the chosen men of Israel, thirty thousand. ² And David arose and went with all the people who were with him from Baale-judah to bring up from there the ark of God, which is called by the name of the LORD of hosts who sits enthroned on the cherubim. ³ And they carried

the ark of God on a new cart and brought it out of the house of Abinadab, which was on the hill. And Uzzah and Ahio, the sons of Abinadab, were driving the new cart, [4] with the ark of God, and Ahio went before the ark.

Uzzah and the Ark

[5] And David and all the house of Israel were celebrating before the LORD, with songs and lyres and harps and tambourines and castanets and cymbals. [6] And when they came to the threshing floor of Nacon, Uzzah put out his hand to the ark of God and took hold of it, for the oxen stumbled. [7] And the anger of the LORD was kindled against Uzzah, and God struck him down there because of his error, and he died there beside the ark of God. [8] And David was angry because the LORD had broken out against Uzzah. And that place is called Perez-uzzah to this day. [9] And David was afraid of the LORD that day, and he said, "How can the ark of the LORD come to me?" [10] So David was not willing to take the ark of the LORD into the city of David. But David took it aside to the house of Obed-edom the Gittite. [11] And the ark of the LORD remained in the house of Obed-edom the Gittite three months, and the LORD blessed Obed-edom and all his household.

[12] And it was told King David, "The LORD has blessed the household of Obed-edom and all that belongs to him, because of the ark of God." So David went and brought up the ark of God from the house of Obed-edom to the city of David with rejoicing. [13] And when those who bore the ark of the LORD had gone six steps, he sacrificed an ox and a fattened animal. [14] And David danced before the LORD with all his might. And David was wearing a linen ephod. [15] So David and all the house of

Israel brought up the ark of the LORD with shouting and with the sound of the horn.

David and Michal

¹⁶ As the ark of the LORD came into the city of David, Michal the daughter of Saul looked out of the window and saw King David leaping and dancing before the LORD, and she despised him in her heart. ¹⁷ And they brought in the ark of the LORD and set it in its place, inside the tent that David had pitched for it. And David offered burnt offerings and peace offerings before the LORD. ¹⁸ And when David had finished offering the burnt offerings and the peace offerings, he blessed the people in the name of the LORD of hosts ¹⁹ and distributed among all the people, the whole multitude of Israel, both men and women, a cake of bread, a portion of meat, and a cake of raisins to each one. Then all the people departed, each to his house.

²⁰ And David returned to bless his household. But Michal the daughter of Saul came out to meet David and said, "How the king of Israel honored himself today, uncovering himself today before the eyes of his servants' female servants, as one of the vulgar fellows shamelessly uncovers himself!" ²¹ And David said to Michal, "It was before the LORD, who chose me above your father and above all his house, to appoint me as prince over Israel, the people of the LORD—and I will celebrate before the LORD. ²² I will make myself yet more contemptible than this, and I will be abased in your eyes. But by the female servants of whom you have spoken, by them I shall be held in honor." ²³ And Michal the daughter of Saul had no child to the day of her death.

The LORD'S *Covenant with David*

7 Now when the king lived in his house and the LORD had given him rest from all his surrounding enemies, ² the king said to Nathan the prophet, "See now, I dwell in a house of cedar, but the ark of God dwells in a tent." ³ And Nathan said to the king, "Go, do all that is in your heart, for the LORD is with you."

⁴ But that same night the word of the LORD came to Nathan, ⁵ "Go and tell my servant David, 'Thus says the LORD: Would you build me a house to dwell in? ⁶ I have not lived in a house since the day I brought up the people of Israel from Egypt to this day, but I have been moving about in a tent for my dwelling. ⁷ In all places where I have moved with all the people of Israel, did I speak a word with any of the judges of Israel, whom I commanded to shepherd my people Israel, saying, "Why have you not built me a house of cedar?"' ⁸ Now, therefore, thus you shall say to my servant David, 'Thus says the LORD of hosts, I took you from the pasture, from following the sheep, that you should be prince over my people Israel. ⁹ And I have been with you wherever you went and have cut off all your enemies from before you. And I will make for you a great name, like the name of the great ones of the earth. ¹⁰ And I will appoint a place for my people Israel and will plant them, so that they may dwell in their own place and be disturbed no more. And violent men shall afflict them no more, as formerly, ¹¹ from the time that I appointed judges over my people Israel. And I will give you rest from all your enemies. Moreover, the LORD declares to you that the LORD will make you a house. ¹² When your days are fulfilled and you lie down with your fathers, I will raise up your offspring after you, who shall come from your body, and I will

establish his kingdom. ¹³ He shall build a house for my name, and I will establish the throne of his kingdom forever. ¹⁴ I will be to him a father, and he shall be to me a son. When he commits iniquity, I will discipline him with the rod of men, with the stripes of the sons of men, ¹⁵ but my steadfast love will not depart from him, as I took it from Saul, whom I put away from before you. ¹⁶ And your house and your kingdom shall be made sure forever before me. Your throne shall be established forever.'" ¹⁷ In accordance with all these words, and in accordance with all this vision, Nathan spoke to David.

David's Prayer of Gratitude

¹⁸ Then King David went in and sat before the LORD and said, "Who am I, O Lord GOD, and what is my house, that you have brought me thus far? ¹⁹ And yet this was a small thing in your eyes, O Lord GOD. You have spoken also of your servant's house for a great while to come, and this is instruction for mankind, O Lord GOD! ²⁰ And what more can David say to you? For you know your servant, O Lord GOD! ²¹ Because of your promise, and according to your own heart, you have brought about all this greatness, to make your servant know it. ²² Therefore you are great, O LORD God. For there is none like you, and there is no God besides you, according to all that we have heard with our ears. ²³ And who is like your people Israel, the one nation on earth whom God went to redeem to be his people, making himself a name and doing for them great and awesome things by driving out before your people, whom you redeemed for yourself from Egypt, a nation and its gods? ²⁴ And you established for yourself your people Israel to be your people forever. And you, O LORD, became their God. ²⁵ And now, O LORD God,

confirm forever the word that you have spoken concerning your servant and concerning his house, and do as you have spoken. ²⁶ And your name will be magnified forever, saying, 'The LORD of hosts is God over Israel,' and the house of your servant David will be established before you. ²⁷ For you, O LORD of hosts, the God of Israel, have made this revelation to your servant, saying, 'I will build you a house.' Therefore your servant has found courage to pray this prayer to you. ²⁸ And now, O Lord GOD, you are God, and your words are true, and you have promised this good thing to your servant. ²⁹ Now therefore may it please you to bless the house of your servant, so that it may continue forever before you. For you, O Lord GOD, have spoken, and with your blessing shall the house of your servant be blessed forever."

David's Victories

8 After this David defeated the Philistines and subdued them, and David took Metheg-ammah out of the hand of the Philistines.

² And he defeated Moab and he measured them with a line, making them lie down on the ground. Two lines he measured to be put to death, and one full line to be spared. And the Moabites became servants to David and brought tribute.

³ David also defeated Hadadezer the son of Rehob, king of Zobah, as he went to restore his power at the river Euphrates. ⁴ And David took from him 1,700 horsemen, and 20,000 foot soldiers. And David hamstrung all the chariot horses but left enough for 100 chariots. ⁵ And when the Syrians of Damascus came to help Hadadezer king of Zobah, David struck down 22,000 men of the Syrians. ⁶ Then David put garrisons in Aram

of Damascus, and the Syrians became servants to David and brought tribute. And the LORD gave victory to David wherever he went. [7] And David took the shields of gold that were carried by the servants of Hadadezer and brought them to Jerusalem. [8] And from Betah and from Berothai, cities of Hadadezer, King David took very much bronze.

[9] When Toi king of Hamath heard that David had defeated the whole army of Hadadezer, [10] Toi sent his son Joram to King David, to ask about his health and to bless him because he had fought against Hadadezer and defeated him, for Hadadezer had often been at war with Toi. And Joram brought with him articles of silver, of gold, and of bronze. [11] These also King David dedicated to the LORD, together with the silver and gold that he dedicated from all the nations he subdued, [12] from Edom, Moab, the Ammonites, the Philistines, Amalek, and from the spoil of Hadadezer the son of Rehob, king of Zobah.

[13] And David made a name for himself when he returned from striking down 18,000 Edomites in the Valley of Salt. [14] Then he put garrisons in Edom; throughout all Edom he put garrisons, and all the Edomites became David's servants. And the LORD gave victory to David wherever he went.

David's Officials

[15] So David reigned over all Israel. And David administered justice and equity to all his people. [16] Joab the son of Zeruiah was over the army, and Jehoshaphat the son of Ahilud was recorder, [17] and Zadok the son of Ahitub and Ahimelech the son of Abiathar were priests, and Seraiah was secretary, [18] and Benaiah the son of Jehoiada was over the Cherethites and the Pelethites, and David's sons were priests.

David's Kindness to Mephibosheth

9 And David said, "Is there still anyone left of the house of Saul, that I may show him kindness for Jonathan's sake?" ²Now there was a servant of the house of Saul whose name was Ziba, and they called him to David. And the king said to him, "Are you Ziba?" And he said, "I am your servant." ³And the king said, "Is there not still someone of the house of Saul, that I may show the kindness of God to him?" Ziba said to the king, "There is still a son of Jonathan; he is crippled in his feet." ⁴The king said to him, "Where is he?" And Ziba said to the king, "He is in the house of Machir the son of Ammiel, at Lo-debar." ⁵Then King David sent and brought him from the house of Machir the son of Ammiel, at Lo-debar. ⁶And Mephibosheth the son of Jonathan, son of Saul, came to David and fell on his face and paid homage. And David said, "Mephibosheth!" And he answered, "Behold, I am your servant." ⁷And David said to him, "Do not fear, for I will show you kindness for the sake of your father Jonathan, and I will restore to you all the land of Saul your father, and you shall eat at my table always." ⁸And he paid homage and said, "What is your servant, that you should show regard for a dead dog such as I?"

⁹Then the king called Ziba, Saul's servant, and said to him, "All that belonged to Saul and to all his house I have given to your master's grandson. ¹⁰And you and your sons and your servants shall till the land for him and shall bring in the produce, that your master's grandson may have bread to eat. But Mephibosheth your master's grandson shall always eat at my table." Now Ziba had fifteen sons and twenty servants. ¹¹Then Ziba said to the king, "According to all that my lord the king commands his servant, so will your servant do."

So Mephibosheth ate at David's table, like one of the king's sons. ¹² And Mephibosheth had a young son, whose name was Mica. And all who lived in Ziba's house became Mephibosheth's servants. ¹³ So Mephibosheth lived in Jerusalem, for he ate always at the king's table. Now he was lame in both his feet.

David Defeats Ammon and Syria

10 After this the king of the Ammonites died, and Hanun his son reigned in his place. ² And David said, "I will deal loyally with Hanun the son of Nahash, as his father dealt loyally with me." So David sent by his servants to console him concerning his father. And David's servants came into the land of the Ammonites. ³ But the princes of the Ammonites said to Hanun their lord, "Do you think, because David has sent comforters to you, that he is honoring your father? Has not David sent his servants to you to search the city and to spy it out and to overthrow it?" ⁴ So Hanun took David's servants and shaved off half the beard of each and cut off their garments in the middle, at their hips, and sent them away. ⁵ When it was told David, he sent to meet them, for the men were greatly ashamed. And the king said, "Remain at Jericho until your beards have grown and then return."

⁶ When the Ammonites saw that they had become a stench to David, the Ammonites sent and hired the Syrians of Bethrehob, and the Syrians of Zobah, 20,000 foot soldiers, and the king of Maacah with 1,000 men, and the men of Tob, 12,000 men. ⁷ And when David heard of it, he sent Joab and all the host of the mighty men. ⁸ And the Ammonites came out and drew up in battle array at the entrance of the gate, and the Syrians of

Zobah and of Rehob and the men of Tob and Maacah were by themselves in the open country.

⁹ When Joab saw that the battle was set against him both in front and in the rear, he chose some of the best men of Israel and arrayed them against the Syrians. ¹⁰ The rest of his men he put in the charge of Abishai his brother, and he arrayed them against the Ammonites. ¹¹ And he said, "If the Syrians are too strong for me, then you shall help me, but if the Ammonites are too strong for you, then I will come and help you. ¹² Be of good courage, and let us be courageous for our people, and for the cities of our God, and may the LORD do what seems good to him." ¹³ So Joab and the people who were with him drew near to battle against the Syrians, and they fled before him. ¹⁴ And when the Ammonites saw that the Syrians fled, they likewise fled before Abishai and entered the city. Then Joab returned from fighting against the Ammonites and came to Jerusalem.

¹⁵ But when the Syrians saw that they had been defeated by Israel, they gathered themselves together. ¹⁶ And Hadadezer sent and brought out the Syrians who were beyond the Euphrates. They came to Helam, with Shobach the commander of the army of Hadadezer at their head. ¹⁷ And when it was told David, he gathered all Israel together and crossed the Jordan and came to Helam. The Syrians arrayed themselves against David and fought with him. ¹⁸ And the Syrians fled before Israel, and David killed of the Syrians the men of 700 chariots, and 40,000 horsemen, and wounded Shobach the commander of their army, so that he died there. ¹⁹ And when all the kings who were servants of Hadadezer saw that they had been defeated by Israel, they made peace with Israel and became subject to them. So the Syrians were afraid to save the Ammonites anymore.

David and Bathsheba

11 In the spring of the year, the time when kings go out to battle, David sent Joab, and his servants with him, and all Israel. And they ravaged the Ammonites and besieged Rabbah. But David remained at Jerusalem.

² It happened, late one afternoon, when David arose from his couch and was walking on the roof of the king's house, that he saw from the roof a woman bathing; and the woman was very beautiful. ³ And David sent and inquired about the woman. And one said, "Is not this Bathsheba, the daughter of Eliam, the wife of Uriah the Hittite?" ⁴ So David sent messengers and took her, and she came to him, and he lay with her. (Now she had been purifying herself from her uncleanness.) Then she returned to her house. ⁵ And the woman conceived, and she sent and told David, "I am pregnant."

⁶ So David sent word to Joab, "Send me Uriah the Hittite." And Joab sent Uriah to David. ⁷ When Uriah came to him, David asked how Joab was doing and how the people were doing and how the war was going. ⁸ Then David said to Uriah, "Go down to your house and wash your feet." And Uriah went out of the king's house, and there followed him a present from the king. ⁹ But Uriah slept at the door of the king's house with all the servants of his lord, and did not go down to his house. ¹⁰ When they told David, "Uriah did not go down to his house," David said to Uriah, "Have you not come from a journey? Why did you not go down to your house?" ¹¹ Uriah said to David, "The ark and Israel and Judah dwell in booths, and my lord Joab and the servants of my lord are camping in the open field. Shall I then go to my house, to eat and to drink and to lie with my wife? As you live, and as your soul lives, I will not do this thing." ¹² Then

David said to Uriah, "Remain here today also, and tomorrow I will send you back." So Uriah remained in Jerusalem that day and the next. ¹³ And David invited him, and he ate in his presence and drank, so that he made him drunk. And in the evening he went out to lie on his couch with the servants of his lord, but he did not go down to his house.

¹⁴ In the morning David wrote a letter to Joab and sent it by the hand of Uriah. ¹⁵ In the letter he wrote, "Set Uriah in the forefront of the hardest fighting, and then draw back from him, that he may be struck down, and die." ¹⁶ And as Joab was besieging the city, he assigned Uriah to the place where he knew there were valiant men. ¹⁷ And the men of the city came out and fought with Joab, and some of the servants of David among the people fell. Uriah the Hittite also died. ¹⁸ Then Joab sent and told David all the news about the fighting. ¹⁹ And he instructed the messenger, "When you have finished telling all the news about the fighting to the king, ²⁰ then, if the king's anger rises, and if he says to you, 'Why did you go so near the city to fight? Did you not know that they would shoot from the wall? ²¹ Who killed Abimelech the son of Jerubbesheth? Did not a woman cast an upper millstone on him from the wall, so that he died at Thebez? Why did you go so near the wall?' then you shall say, 'Your servant Uriah the Hittite is dead also.'"

²² So the messenger went and came and told David all that Joab had sent him to tell. ²³ The messenger said to David, "The men gained an advantage over us and came out against us in the field, but we drove them back to the entrance of the gate. ²⁴ Then the archers shot at your servants from the wall. Some of the king's servants are dead, and your servant Uriah the Hittite is dead also." ²⁵ David said to the messenger, "Thus shall you

say to Joab, 'Do not let this matter displease you, for the sword devours now one and now another. Strengthen your attack against the city and overthrow it.' And encourage him."

²⁶ When the wife of Uriah heard that Uriah her husband was dead, she lamented over her husband. ²⁷ And when the mourning was over, David sent and brought her to his house, and she became his wife and bore him a son. But the thing that David had done displeased the LORD.

Nathan Rebukes David

12 And the LORD sent Nathan to David. He came to him and said to him, "There were two men in a certain city, the one rich and the other poor. ² The rich man had very many flocks and herds, ³ but the poor man had nothing but one little ewe lamb, which he had bought. And he brought it up, and it grew up with him and with his children. It used to eat of his morsel and drink from his cup and lie in his arms, and it was like a daughter to him. ⁴ Now there came a traveler to the rich man, and he was unwilling to take one of his own flock or herd to prepare for the guest who had come to him, but he took the poor man's lamb and prepared it for the man who had come to him." ⁵ Then David's anger was greatly kindled against the man, and he said to Nathan, "As the LORD lives, the man who has done this deserves to die, ⁶ and he shall restore the lamb fourfold, because he did this thing, and because he had no pity."

⁷ Nathan said to David, "You are the man! Thus says the LORD, the God of Israel, 'I anointed you king over Israel, and I delivered you out of the hand of Saul. ⁸ And I gave you your master's house and your master's wives into your arms and

gave you the house of Israel and of Judah. And if this were too little, I would add to you as much more. ⁹ Why have you despised the word of the LORD, to do what is evil in his sight? You have struck down Uriah the Hittite with the sword and have taken his wife to be your wife and have killed him with the sword of the Ammonites. ¹⁰ Now therefore the sword shall never depart from your house, because you have despised me and have taken the wife of Uriah the Hittite to be your wife.' ¹¹ Thus says the LORD, 'Behold, I will raise up evil against you out of your own house. And I will take your wives before your eyes and give them to your neighbor, and he shall lie with your wives in the sight of this sun. ¹² For you did it secretly, but I will do this thing before all Israel and before the sun.'" ¹³ David said to Nathan, "I have sinned against the LORD." And Nathan said to David, "The LORD also has put away your sin; you shall not die. ¹⁴ Nevertheless, because by this deed you have utterly scorned the LORD, the child who is born to you shall die." ¹⁵ Then Nathan went to his house.

David's Child Dies

And the LORD afflicted the child that Uriah's wife bore to David, and he became sick. ¹⁶ David therefore sought God on behalf of the child. And David fasted and went in and lay all night on the ground. ¹⁷ And the elders of his house stood beside him, to raise him from the ground, but he would not, nor did he eat food with them. ¹⁸ On the seventh day the child died. And the servants of David were afraid to tell him that the child was dead, for they said, "Behold, while the child was yet alive, we spoke to him, and he did not listen to us. How then can we say to him the child is dead? He may do himself some

harm." [19] But when David saw that his servants were whispering together, David understood that the child was dead. And David said to his servants, "Is the child dead?" They said, "He is dead." [20] Then David arose from the earth and washed and anointed himself and changed his clothes. And he went into the house of the LORD and worshiped. He then went to his own house. And when he asked, they set food before him, and he ate. [21] Then his servants said to him, "What is this thing that you have done? You fasted and wept for the child while he was alive; but when the child died, you arose and ate food." [22] He said, "While the child was still alive, I fasted and wept, for I said, 'Who knows whether the LORD will be gracious to me, that the child may live?' [23] But now he is dead. Why should I fast? Can I bring him back again? I shall go to him, but he will not return to me."

Solomon's Birth

[24] Then David comforted his wife, Bathsheba, and went in to her and lay with her, and she bore a son, and he called his name Solomon. And the LORD loved him [25] and sent a message by Nathan the prophet. So he called his name Jedidiah, because of the LORD.

Rabbah Is Captured

[26] Now Joab fought against Rabbah of the Ammonites and took the royal city. [27] And Joab sent messengers to David and said, "I have fought against Rabbah; moreover, I have taken the city of waters. [28] Now then gather the rest of the people together and encamp against the city and take it, lest I take the city and it be called by my name." [29] So David gathered all the people together and went to Rabbah and fought against it and

took it. ³⁰ And he took the crown of their king from his head. The weight of it was a talent of gold, and in it was a precious stone, and it was placed on David's head. And he brought out the spoil of the city, a very great amount. ³¹ And he brought out the people who were in it and set them to labor with saws and iron picks and iron axes and made them toil at the brick kilns. And thus he did to all the cities of the Ammonites. Then David and all the people returned to Jerusalem.

Amnon and Tamar

13 Now Absalom, David's son, had a beautiful sister, whose name was Tamar. And after a time Amnon, David's son, loved her. ² And Amnon was so tormented that he made himself ill because of his sister Tamar, for she was a virgin, and it seemed impossible to Amnon to do anything to her. ³ But Amnon had a friend, whose name was Jonadab, the son of Shimeah, David's brother. And Jonadab was a very crafty man. ⁴ And he said to him, "O son of the king, why are you so haggard morning after morning? Will you not tell me?" Amnon said to him, "I love Tamar, my brother Absalom's sister." ⁵ Jonadab said to him, "Lie down on your bed and pretend to be ill. And when your father comes to see you, say to him, 'Let my sister Tamar come and give me bread to eat, and prepare the food in my sight, that I may see it and eat it from her hand.'" ⁶ So Amnon lay down and pretended to be ill. And when the king came to see him, Amnon said to the king, "Please let my sister Tamar come and make a couple of cakes in my sight, that I may eat from her hand."

⁷ Then David sent home to Tamar, saying, "Go to your brother Amnon's house and prepare food for him." ⁸ So Tamar

went to her brother Amnon's house, where he was lying down. And she took dough and kneaded it and made cakes in his sight and baked the cakes. ⁹ And she took the pan and emptied it out before him, but he refused to eat. And Amnon said, "Send out everyone from me." So everyone went out from him. ¹⁰ Then Amnon said to Tamar, "Bring the food into the chamber, that I may eat from your hand." And Tamar took the cakes she had made and brought them into the chamber to Amnon her brother. ¹¹ But when she brought them near him to eat, he took hold of her and said to her, "Come, lie with me, my sister." ¹² She answered him, "No, my brother, do not violate me, for such a thing is not done in Israel; do not do this outrageous thing. ¹³ As for me, where could I carry my shame? And as for you, you would be as one of the outrageous fools in Israel. Now therefore, please speak to the king, for he will not withhold me from you." ¹⁴ But he would not listen to her, and being stronger than she, he violated her and lay with her.

¹⁵ Then Amnon hated her with very great hatred, so that the hatred with which he hated her was greater than the love with which he had loved her. And Amnon said to her, "Get up! Go!" ¹⁶ But she said to him, "No, my brother, for this wrong in sending me away is greater than the other that you did to me." But he would not listen to her. ¹⁷ He called the young man who served him and said, "Put this woman out of my presence and bolt the door after her." ¹⁸ Now she was wearing a long robe with sleeves, for thus were the virgin daughters of the king dressed. So his servant put her out and bolted the door after her. ¹⁹ And Tamar put ashes on her head and tore the long robe that she wore. And she laid her hand on her head and went away, crying aloud as she went.

²⁰ And her brother Absalom said to her, "Has Amnon your brother been with you? Now hold your peace, my sister. He is your brother; do not take this to heart." So Tamar lived, a desolate woman, in her brother Absalom's house. ²¹ When King David heard of all these things, he was very angry. ²² But Absalom spoke to Amnon neither good nor bad, for Absalom hated Amnon, because he had violated his sister Tamar.

Absalom Murders Amnon

²³ After two full years Absalom had sheepshearers at Baal-hazor, which is near Ephraim, and Absalom invited all the king's sons. ²⁴ And Absalom came to the king and said, "Behold, your servant has sheepshearers. Please let the king and his servants go with your servant." ²⁵ But the king said to Absalom, "No, my son, let us not all go, lest we be burdensome to you." He pressed him, but he would not go but gave him his blessing. ²⁶ Then Absalom said, "If not, please let my brother Amnon go with us." And the king said to him, "Why should he go with you?" ²⁷ But Absalom pressed him until he let Amnon and all the king's sons go with him. ²⁸ Then Absalom commanded his servants, "Mark when Amnon's heart is merry with wine, and when I say to you, 'Strike Amnon,' then kill him. Do not fear; have I not commanded you? Be courageous and be valiant." ²⁹ So the servants of Absalom did to Amnon as Absalom had commanded. Then all the king's sons arose, and each mounted his mule and fled.

³⁰ While they were on the way, news came to David, "Absalom has struck down all the king's sons, and not one of them is left." ³¹ Then the king arose and tore his garments and lay on the earth. And all his servants who were standing by tore their

garments. ³² But Jonadab the son of Shimeah, David's brother, said, "Let not my lord suppose that they have killed all the young men, the king's sons, for Amnon alone is dead. For by the command of Absalom this has been determined from the day he violated his sister Tamar. ³³ Now therefore let not my lord the king so take it to heart as to suppose that all the king's sons are dead, for Amnon alone is dead."

Absalom Flees to Geshur

³⁴ But Absalom fled. And the young man who kept the watch lifted up his eyes and looked, and behold, many people were coming from the road behind him by the side of the mountain. ³⁵ And Jonadab said to the king, "Behold, the king's sons have come; as your servant said, so it has come about." ³⁶ And as soon as he had finished speaking, behold, the king's sons came and lifted up their voice and wept. And the king also and all his servants wept very bitterly.

³⁷ But Absalom fled and went to Talmai the son of Ammihud, king of Geshur. And David mourned for his son day after day. ³⁸ So Absalom fled and went to Geshur, and was there three years. ³⁹ And the spirit of the king longed to go out to Absalom, because he was comforted about Amnon, since he was dead.

Absalom Returns to Jerusalem

14 Now Joab the son of Zeruiah knew that the king's heart went out to Absalom. ² And Joab sent to Tekoa and brought from there a wise woman and said to her, "Pretend to be a mourner and put on mourning garments. Do not anoint yourself with oil, but behave like a woman who has been

mourning many days for the dead. ³ Go to the king and speak thus to him." So Joab put the words in her mouth.

⁴ When the woman of Tekoa came to the king, she fell on her face to the ground and paid homage and said, "Save me, O king." ⁵ And the king said to her, "What is your trouble?" She answered, "Alas, I am a widow; my husband is dead. ⁶ And your servant had two sons, and they quarreled with one another in the field. There was no one to separate them, and one struck the other and killed him. ⁷ And now the whole clan has risen against your servant, and they say, 'Give up the man who struck his brother, that we may put him to death for the life of his brother whom he killed.' And so they would destroy the heir also. Thus they would quench my coal that is left and leave to my husband neither name nor remnant on the face of the earth."

⁸ Then the king said to the woman, "Go to your house, and I will give orders concerning you." ⁹ And the woman of Tekoa said to the king, "On me be the guilt, my lord the king, and on my father's house; let the king and his throne be guiltless." ¹⁰ The king said, "If anyone says anything to you, bring him to me, and he shall never touch you again." ¹¹ Then she said, "Please let the king invoke the LORD your God, that the avenger of blood kill no more, and my son be not destroyed." He said, "As the LORD lives, not one hair of your son shall fall to the ground."

¹² Then the woman said, "Please let your servant speak a word to my lord the king." He said, "Speak." ¹³ And the woman said, "Why then have you planned such a thing against the people of God? For in giving this decision the king convicts himself, inasmuch as the king does not bring his banished one home again. ¹⁴ We must all die; we are like water spilled on the ground, which cannot be gathered up again. But God will not

take away life, and he devises means so that the banished one will not remain an outcast. ¹⁵ Now I have come to say this to my lord the king because the people have made me afraid, and your servant thought, 'I will speak to the king; it may be that the king will perform the request of his servant. ¹⁶ For the king will hear and deliver his servant from the hand of the man who would destroy me and my son together from the heritage of God.' ¹⁷ And your servant thought, 'The word of my lord the king will set me at rest,' for my lord the king is like the angel of God to discern good and evil. The LORD your God be with you!"

¹⁸ Then the king answered the woman, "Do not hide from me anything I ask you." And the woman said, "Let my lord the king speak." ¹⁹ The king said, "Is the hand of Joab with you in all this?" The woman answered and said, "As surely as you live, my lord the king, one cannot turn to the right hand or to the left from anything that my lord the king has said. It was your servant Joab who commanded me; it was he who put all these words in the mouth of your servant. ²⁰ In order to change the course of things your servant Joab did this. But my lord has wisdom like the wisdom of the angel of God to know all things that are on the earth."

²¹ Then the king said to Joab, "Behold now, I grant this; go, bring back the young man Absalom." ²² And Joab fell on his face to the ground and paid homage and blessed the king. And Joab said, "Today your servant knows that I have found favor in your sight, my lord the king, in that the king has granted the request of his servant." ²³ So Joab arose and went to Geshur and brought Absalom to Jerusalem. ²⁴ And the king said, "Let him dwell apart in his own house; he is not to come into my presence." So Absalom lived apart in his own house and did not come into the king's presence.

²⁵ Now in all Israel there was no one so much to be praised for his handsome appearance as Absalom. From the sole of his foot to the crown of his head there was no blemish in him. ²⁶ And when he cut the hair of his head (for at the end of every year he used to cut it; when it was heavy on him, he cut it), he weighed the hair of his head, two hundred shekels by the king's weight. ²⁷ There were born to Absalom three sons, and one daughter whose name was Tamar. She was a beautiful woman.

²⁸ So Absalom lived two full years in Jerusalem, without coming into the king's presence. ²⁹ Then Absalom sent for Joab, to send him to the king, but Joab would not come to him. And he sent a second time, but Joab would not come. ³⁰ Then he said to his servants, "See, Joab's field is next to mine, and he has barley there; go and set it on fire." So Absalom's servants set the field on fire. ³¹ Then Joab arose and went to Absalom at his house and said to him, "Why have your servants set my field on fire?" ³² Absalom answered Joab, "Behold, I sent word to you, 'Come here, that I may send you to the king, to ask, "Why have I come from Geshur? It would be better for me to be there still."' Now therefore let me go into the presence of the king, and if there is guilt in me, let him put me to death.'" ³³ Then Joab went to the king and told him, and he summoned Absalom. So he came to the king and bowed himself on his face to the ground before the king, and the king kissed Absalom.

Absalom's Conspiracy

15 After this Absalom got himself a chariot and horses, and fifty men to run before him. ² And Absalom used to rise early and stand beside the way of the gate. And when any man had a dispute to come before the king for judgment, Absalom

would call to him and say, "From what city are you?" And when he said, "Your servant is of such and such a tribe in Israel," ³ Absalom would say to him, "See, your claims are good and right, but there is no man designated by the king to hear you." ⁴ Then Absalom would say, "Oh that I were judge in the land! Then every man with a dispute or cause might come to me, and I would give him justice." ⁵ And whenever a man came near to pay homage to him, he would put out his hand and take hold of him and kiss him. ⁶ Thus Absalom did to all of Israel who came to the king for judgment. So Absalom stole the hearts of the men of Israel.

⁷ And at the end of four years Absalom said to the king, "Please let me go and pay my vow, which I have vowed to the LORD, in Hebron. ⁸ For your servant vowed a vow while I lived at Geshur in Aram, saying, 'If the LORD will indeed bring me back to Jerusalem, then I will offer worship to the LORD.'" ⁹ The king said to him, "Go in peace." So he arose and went to Hebron. ¹⁰ But Absalom sent secret messengers throughout all the tribes of Israel, saying, "As soon as you hear the sound of the trumpet, then say, 'Absalom is king at Hebron!'" ¹¹ With Absalom went two hundred men from Jerusalem who were invited guests, and they went in their innocence and knew nothing. ¹² And while Absalom was offering the sacrifices, he sent for Ahithophel the Gilonite, David's counselor, from his city Giloh. And the conspiracy grew strong, and the people with Absalom kept increasing.

David Flees Jerusalem

¹³ And a messenger came to David, saying, "The hearts of the men of Israel have gone after Absalom." ¹⁴ Then David said

to all his servants who were with him at Jerusalem, "Arise, and let us flee, or else there will be no escape for us from Absalom. Go quickly, lest he overtake us quickly and bring down ruin on us and strike the city with the edge of the sword." ¹⁵ And the king's servants said to the king, "Behold, your servants are ready to do whatever my lord the king decides." ¹⁶ So the king went out, and all his household after him. And the king left ten concubines to keep the house. ¹⁷ And the king went out, and all the people after him. And they halted at the last house.

¹⁸ And all his servants passed by him, and all the Cherethites, and all the Pelethites, and all the six hundred Gittites who had followed him from Gath, passed on before the king. ¹⁹ Then the king said to Ittai the Gittite, "Why do you also go with us? Go back and stay with the king, for you are a foreigner and also an exile from your home. ²⁰ You came only yesterday, and shall I today make you wander about with us, since I go I know not where? Go back and take your brothers with you, and may the LORD show steadfast love and faithfulness to you." ²¹ But Ittai answered the king, "As the LORD lives, and as my lord the king lives, wherever my lord the king shall be, whether for death or for life, there also will your servant be." ²² And David said to Ittai, "Go then, pass on." So Ittai the Gittite passed on with all his men and all the little ones who were with him. ²³ And all the land wept aloud as all the people passed by, and the king crossed the brook Kidron, and all the people passed on toward the wilderness.

²⁴ And Abiathar came up, and behold, Zadok came also with all the Levites, bearing the ark of the covenant of God. And they set down the ark of God until the people had all passed out of the city. ²⁵ Then the king said to Zadok, "Carry the ark of God back

into the city. If I find favor in the eyes of the LORD, he will bring me back and let me see both it and his dwelling place. ²⁶ But if he says, 'I have no pleasure in you,' behold, here I am, let him do to me what seems good to him." ²⁷ The king also said to Zadok the priest, "Are you not a seer? Go back to the city in peace, with your two sons, Ahimaaz your son, and Jonathan the son of Abiathar. ²⁸ See, I will wait at the fords of the wilderness until word comes from you to inform me." ²⁹ So Zadok and Abiathar carried the ark of God back to Jerusalem, and they remained there.

³⁰ But David went up the ascent of the Mount of Olives, weeping as he went, barefoot and with his head covered. And all the people who were with him covered their heads, and they went up, weeping as they went. ³¹ And it was told David, "Ahithophel is among the conspirators with Absalom." And David said, "O LORD, please turn the counsel of Ahithophel into foolishness."

³² While David was coming to the summit, where God was worshiped, behold, Hushai the Archite came to meet him with his coat torn and dirt on his head. ³³ David said to him, "If you go on with me, you will be a burden to me. ³⁴ But if you return to the city and say to Absalom, 'I will be your servant, O king; as I have been your father's servant in time past, so now I will be your servant,' then you will defeat for me the counsel of Ahithophel. ³⁵ Are not Zadok and Abiathar the priests with you there? So whatever you hear from the king's house, tell it to Zadok and Abiathar the priests. ³⁶ Behold, their two sons are with them there, Ahimaaz, Zadok's son, and Jonathan, Abiathar's son, and by them you shall send to me everything you hear." ³⁷ So Hushai, David's friend, came into the city, just as Absalom was entering Jerusalem.

David and Ziba

16 When David had passed a little beyond the summit, Ziba the servant of Mephibosheth met him, with a couple of donkeys saddled, bearing two hundred loaves of bread, a hundred bunches of raisins, a hundred of summer fruits, and a skin of wine. ²And the king said to Ziba, "Why have you brought these?" Ziba answered, "The donkeys are for the king's household to ride on, the bread and summer fruit for the young men to eat, and the wine for those who faint in the wilderness to drink." ³And the king said, "And where is your master's son?" Ziba said to the king, "Behold, he remains in Jerusalem, for he said, 'Today the house of Israel will give me back the kingdom of my father.'" ⁴Then the king said to Ziba, "Behold, all that belonged to Mephibosheth is now yours." And Ziba said, "I pay homage; let me ever find favor in your sight, my lord the king."

Shimei Curses David

⁵When King David came to Bahurim, there came out a man of the family of the house of Saul, whose name was Shimei, the son of Gera, and as he came he cursed continually. ⁶And he threw stones at David and at all the servants of King David, and all the people and all the mighty men were on his right hand and on his left. ⁷And Shimei said as he cursed, "Get out, get out, you man of blood, you worthless man! ⁸The LORD has avenged on you all the blood of the house of Saul, in whose place you have reigned, and the LORD has given the kingdom into the hand of your son Absalom. See, your evil is on you, for you are a man of blood."

⁹Then Abishai the son of Zeruiah said to the king, "Why should this dead dog curse my lord the king? Let me go over

and take off his head." [10] But the king said, "What have I to do with you, you sons of Zeruiah? If he is cursing because the LORD has said to him, 'Curse David,' who then shall say, 'Why have you done so?'" [11] And David said to Abishai and to all his servants, "Behold, my own son seeks my life; how much more now may this Benjaminite! Leave him alone, and let him curse, for the LORD has told him to. [12] It may be that the LORD will look on the wrong done to me, and that the LORD will repay me with good for his cursing today." [13] So David and his men went on the road, while Shimei went along on the hillside opposite him and cursed as he went and threw stones at him and flung dust. [14] And the king, and all the people who were with him, arrived weary at the Jordan. And there he refreshed himself.

Absalom Enters Jerusalem

[15] Now Absalom and all the people, the men of Israel, came to Jerusalem, and Ahithophel with him. [16] And when Hushai the Archite, David's friend, came to Absalom, Hushai said to Absalom, "Long live the king! Long live the king!" [17] And Absalom said to Hushai, "Is this your loyalty to your friend? Why did you not go with your friend?" [18] And Hushai said to Absalom, "No, for whom the LORD and this people and all the men of Israel have chosen, his I will be, and with him I will remain. [19] And again, whom should I serve? Should it not be his son? As I have served your father, so I will serve you."

[20] Then Absalom said to Ahithophel, "Give your counsel. What shall we do?" [21] Ahithophel said to Absalom, "Go in to your father's concubines, whom he has left to keep the house, and all Israel will hear that you have made yourself a

stench to your father, and the hands of all who are with you will be strengthened." ²² So they pitched a tent for Absalom on the roof. And Absalom went in to his father's concubines in the sight of all Israel. ²³ Now in those days the counsel that Ahithophel gave was as if one consulted the word of God; so was all the counsel of Ahithophel esteemed, both by David and by Absalom.

Hushai Saves David

17 Moreover, Ahithophel said to Absalom, "Let me choose twelve thousand men, and I will arise and pursue David tonight. ² I will come upon him while he is weary and discouraged and throw him into a panic, and all the people who are with him will flee. I will strike down only the king, ³ and I will bring all the people back to you as a bride comes home to her husband. You seek the life of only one man, and all the people will be at peace." ⁴ And the advice seemed right in the eyes of Absalom and all the elders of Israel.

⁵ Then Absalom said, "Call Hushai the Archite also, and let us hear what he has to say." ⁶ And when Hushai came to Absalom, Absalom said to him, "Thus has Ahithophel spoken; shall we do as he says? If not, you speak." ⁷ Then Hushai said to Absalom, "This time the counsel that Ahithophel has given is not good." ⁸ Hushai said, "You know that your father and his men are mighty men, and that they are enraged, like a bear robbed of her cubs in the field. Besides, your father is expert in war; he will not spend the night with the people. ⁹ Behold, even now he has hidden himself in one of the pits or in some other place. And as soon as some of the people fall at the first attack, whoever hears it will say, 'There has been

a slaughter among the people who follow Absalom.' [10] Then even the valiant man, whose heart is like the heart of a lion, will utterly melt with fear, for all Israel knows that your father is a mighty man, and that those who are with him are valiant men. [11] But my counsel is that all Israel be gathered to you, from Dan to Beersheba, as the sand by the sea for multitude, and that you go to battle in person. [12] So we shall come upon him in some place where he is to be found, and we shall light upon him as the dew falls on the ground, and of him and all the men with him not one will be left. [13] If he withdraws into a city, then all Israel will bring ropes to that city, and we shall drag it into the valley, until not even a pebble is to be found there." [14] And Absalom and all the men of Israel said, "The counsel of Hushai the Archite is better than the counsel of Ahithophel." For the LORD had ordained to defeat the good counsel of Ahithophel, so that the LORD might bring harm upon Absalom.

[15] Then Hushai said to Zadok and Abiathar the priests, "Thus and so did Ahithophel counsel Absalom and the elders of Israel, and thus and so have I counseled. [16] Now therefore send quickly and tell David, 'Do not stay tonight at the fords of the wilderness, but by all means pass over, lest the king and all the people who are with him be swallowed up.'" [17] Now Jonathan and Ahimaaz were waiting at En-rogel. A female servant was to go and tell them, and they were to go and tell King David, for they were not to be seen entering the city. [18] But a young man saw them and told Absalom. So both of them went away quickly and came to the house of a man at Bahurim, who had a well in his courtyard. And they went down into it. [19] And the woman took and spread a covering over the well's mouth

and scattered grain on it, and nothing was known of it. ²⁰ When Absalom's servants came to the woman at the house, they said, "Where are Ahimaaz and Jonathan?" And the woman said to them, "They have gone over the brook of water." And when they had sought and could not find them, they returned to Jerusalem.

²¹ After they had gone, the men came up out of the well, and went and told King David. They said to David, "Arise, and go quickly over the water, for thus and so has Ahithophel counseled against you." ²² Then David arose, and all the people who were with him, and they crossed the Jordan. By daybreak not one was left who had not crossed the Jordan.

²³ When Ahithophel saw that his counsel was not followed, he saddled his donkey and went off home to his own city. He set his house in order and hanged himself, and he died and was buried in the tomb of his father.

²⁴ Then David came to Mahanaim. And Absalom crossed the Jordan with all the men of Israel. ²⁵ Now Absalom had set Amasa over the army instead of Joab. Amasa was the son of a man named Ithra the Ishmaelite, who had married Abigal the daughter of Nahash, sister of Zeruiah, Joab's mother. ²⁶ And Israel and Absalom encamped in the land of Gilead.

²⁷ When David came to Mahanaim, Shobi the son of Nahash from Rabbah of the Ammonites, and Machir the son of Ammiel from Lo-debar, and Barzillai the Gileadite from Rogelim, ²⁸ brought beds, basins, and earthen vessels, wheat, barley, flour, parched grain, beans and lentils, ²⁹ honey and curds and sheep and cheese from the herd, for David and the people with him to eat, for they said, "The people are hungry and weary and thirsty in the wilderness."

Absalom Killed

18
Then David mustered the men who were with him and set over them commanders of thousands and commanders of hundreds. ² And David sent out the army, one third under the command of Joab, one third under the command of Abishai the son of Zeruiah, Joab's brother, and one third under the command of Ittai the Gittite. And the king said to the men, "I myself will also go out with you." ³ But the men said, "You shall not go out. For if we flee, they will not care about us. If half of us die, they will not care about us. But you are worth ten thousand of us. Therefore it is better that you send us help from the city." ⁴ The king said to them, "Whatever seems best to you I will do." So the king stood at the side of the gate, while all the army marched out by hundreds and by thousands. ⁵ And the king ordered Joab and Abishai and Ittai, "Deal gently for my sake with the young man Absalom." And all the people heard when the king gave orders to all the commanders about Absalom.

⁶ So the army went out into the field against Israel, and the battle was fought in the forest of Ephraim. ⁷ And the men of Israel were defeated there by the servants of David, and the loss there was great on that day, twenty thousand men. ⁸ The battle spread over the face of all the country, and the forest devoured more people that day than the sword.

⁹ And Absalom happened to meet the servants of David. Absalom was riding on his mule, and the mule went under the thick branches of a great oak, and his head caught fast in the oak, and he was suspended between heaven and earth, while the mule that was under him went on. ¹⁰ And a certain man saw it and told Joab, "Behold, I saw Absalom hanging in an oak."

¹¹ Joab said to the man who told him, "What, you saw him! Why then did you not strike him there to the ground? I would have been glad to give you ten pieces of silver and a belt." ¹² But the man said to Joab, "Even if I felt in my hand the weight of a thousand pieces of silver, I would not reach out my hand against the king's son, for in our hearing the king commanded you and Abishai and Ittai, 'For my sake protect the young man Absalom.' ¹³ On the other hand, if I had dealt treacherously against his life (and there is nothing hidden from the king), then you yourself would have stood aloof." ¹⁴ Joab said, "I will not waste time like this with you." And he took three javelins in his hand and thrust them into the heart of Absalom while he was still alive in the oak. ¹⁵ And ten young men, Joab's armor-bearers, surrounded Absalom and struck him and killed him.

¹⁶ Then Joab blew the trumpet, and the troops came back from pursuing Israel, for Joab restrained them. ¹⁷ And they took Absalom and threw him into a great pit in the forest and raised over him a very great heap of stones. And all Israel fled every one to his own home. ¹⁸ Now Absalom in his lifetime had taken and set up for himself the pillar that is in the King's Valley, for he said, "I have no son to keep my name in remembrance." He called the pillar after his own name, and it is called Absalom's monument to this day.

David Hears of Absalom's Death

¹⁹ Then Ahimaaz the son of Zadok said, "Let me run and carry news to the king that the LORD has delivered him from the hand of his enemies." ²⁰ And Joab said to him, "You are not to carry news today. You may carry news another day, but today you shall carry no news, because the king's son is dead." ²¹ Then

Joab said to the Cushite, "Go, tell the king what you have seen." The Cushite bowed before Joab, and ran. ²² Then Ahimaaz the son of Zadok said again to Joab, "Come what may, let me also run after the Cushite." And Joab said, "Why will you run, my son, seeing that you will have no reward for the news?" ²³ "Come what may," he said, "I will run." So he said to him, "Run." Then Ahimaaz ran by the way of the plain, and outran the Cushite.

²⁴ Now David was sitting between the two gates, and the watchman went up to the roof of the gate by the wall, and when he lifted up his eyes and looked, he saw a man running alone. ²⁵ The watchman called out and told the king. And the king said, "If he is alone, there is news in his mouth." And he drew nearer and nearer. ²⁶ The watchman saw another man running. And the watchman called to the gate and said, "See, another man running alone!" The king said, "He also brings news." ²⁷ The watchman said, "I think the running of the first is like the running of Ahimaaz the son of Zadok." And the king said, "He is a good man and comes with good news."

²⁸ Then Ahimaaz cried out to the king, "All is well." And he bowed before the king with his face to the earth and said, "Blessed be the LORD your God, who has delivered up the men who raised their hand against my lord the king." ²⁹ And the king said, "Is it well with the young man Absalom?" Ahimaaz answered, "When Joab sent the king's servant, your servant, I saw a great commotion, but I do not know what it was." ³⁰ And the king said, "Turn aside and stand here." So he turned aside and stood still.

David's Grief

³¹ And behold, the Cushite came, and the Cushite said, "Good news for my lord the king! For the LORD has delivered

you this day from the hand of all who rose up against you."
³² The king said to the Cushite, "Is it well with the young man
Absalom?" And the Cushite answered, "May the enemies of my
lord the king and all who rise up against you for evil be like that
young man." ³³ And the king was deeply moved and went up to
the chamber over the gate and wept. And as he went, he said,
"O my son Absalom, my son, my son Absalom! Would I had
died instead of you, O Absalom, my son, my son!"

Joab Rebukes David

19 It was told Joab, "Behold, the king is weeping and
mourning for Absalom." ² So the victory that day was
turned into mourning for all the people, for the people heard
that day, "The king is grieving for his son." ³ And the people
stole into the city that day as people steal in who are ashamed
when they flee in battle. ⁴ The king covered his face, and the
king cried with a loud voice, "O my son Absalom, O Absalom,
my son, my son!" ⁵ Then Joab came into the house to the king
and said, "You have today covered with shame the faces of all
your servants, who have this day saved your life and the lives
of your sons and your daughters and the lives of your wives
and your concubines, ⁶ because you love those who hate you
and hate those who love you. For you have made it clear today
that commanders and servants are nothing to you, for today I
know that if Absalom were alive and all of us were dead today,
then you would be pleased. ⁷ Now therefore arise, go out and
speak kindly to your servants, for I swear by the LORD, if you
do not go, not a man will stay with you this night, and this will
be worse for you than all the evil that has come upon you from
your youth until now." ⁸ Then the king arose and took his seat

in the gate. And the people were all told, "Behold, the king is sitting in the gate." And all the people came before the king.

David Returns to Jerusalem

Now Israel had fled every man to his own home. ⁹ And all the people were arguing throughout all the tribes of Israel, saying, "The king delivered us from the hand of our enemies and saved us from the hand of the Philistines, and now he has fled out of the land from Absalom. ¹⁰ But Absalom, whom we anointed over us, is dead in battle. Now therefore why do you say nothing about bringing the king back?"

¹¹ And King David sent this message to Zadok and Abiathar the priests: "Say to the elders of Judah, 'Why should you be the last to bring the king back to his house, when the word of all Israel has come to the king? ¹² You are my brothers; you are my bone and my flesh. Why then should you be the last to bring back the king?' ¹³ And say to Amasa, 'Are you not my bone and my flesh? God do so to me and more also, if you are not commander of my army from now on in place of Joab.'" ¹⁴ And he swayed the heart of all the men of Judah as one man, so that they sent word to the king, "Return, both you and all your servants." ¹⁵ So the king came back to the Jordan, and Judah came to Gilgal to meet the king and to bring the king over the Jordan.

David Pardons His Enemies

¹⁶ And Shimei the son of Gera, the Benjaminite, from Bahurim, hurried to come down with the men of Judah to meet King David. ¹⁷ And with him were a thousand men from Benjamin. And Ziba the servant of the house of Saul, with his fifteen sons and his twenty servants, rushed down to the Jordan

before the king, [18] and they crossed the ford to bring over the king's household and to do his pleasure. And Shimei the son of Gera fell down before the king, as he was about to cross the Jordan, [19] and said to the king, "Let not my lord hold me guilty or remember how your servant did wrong on the day my lord the king left Jerusalem. Do not let the king take it to heart. [20] For your servant knows that I have sinned. Therefore, behold, I have come this day, the first of all the house of Joseph to come down to meet my lord the king." [21] Abishai the son of Zeruiah answered, "Shall not Shimei be put to death for this, because he cursed the LORD's anointed?" [22] But David said, "What have I to do with you, you sons of Zeruiah, that you should this day be as an adversary to me? Shall anyone be put to death in Israel this day? For do I not know that I am this day king over Israel?" [23] And the king said to Shimei, "You shall not die." And the king gave him his oath.

[24] And Mephibosheth the son of Saul came down to meet the king. He had neither taken care of his feet nor trimmed his beard nor washed his clothes, from the day the king departed until the day he came back in safety. [25] And when he came to Jerusalem to meet the king, the king said to him, "Why did you not go with me, Mephibosheth?" [26] He answered, "My lord, O king, my servant deceived me, for your servant said to him, 'I will saddle a donkey for myself, that I may ride on it and go with the king.' For your servant is lame. [27] He has slandered your servant to my lord the king. But my lord the king is like the angel of God; do therefore what seems good to you. [28] For all my father's house were but men doomed to death before my lord the king, but you set your servant among those who eat at your table. What further right have I, then, to cry to the

king?" ²⁹ And the king said to him, "Why speak any more of your affairs? I have decided: you and Ziba shall divide the land." ³⁰ And Mephibosheth said to the king, "Oh, let him take it all, since my lord the king has come safely home."

³¹ Now Barzillai the Gileadite had come down from Rogelim, and he went on with the king to the Jordan, to escort him over the Jordan. ³² Barzillai was a very aged man, eighty years old. He had provided the king with food while he stayed at Mahanaim, for he was a very wealthy man. ³³ And the king said to Barzillai, "Come over with me, and I will provide for you with me in Jerusalem." ³⁴ But Barzillai said to the king, "How many years have I still to live, that I should go up with the king to Jerusalem? ³⁵ I am this day eighty years old. Can I discern what is pleasant and what is not? Can your servant taste what he eats or what he drinks? Can I still listen to the voice of singing men and singing women? Why then should your servant be an added burden to my lord the king? ³⁶ Your servant will go a little way over the Jordan with the king. Why should the king repay me with such a reward? ³⁷ Please let your servant return, that I may die in my own city near the grave of my father and my mother. But here is your servant Chimham. Let him go over with my lord the king, and do for him whatever seems good to you." ³⁸ And the king answered, "Chimham shall go over with me, and I will do for him whatever seems good to you, and all that you desire of me I will do for you." ³⁹ Then all the people went over the Jordan, and the king went over. And the king kissed Barzillai and blessed him, and he returned to his own home. ⁴⁰ The king went on to Gilgal, and Chimham went on with him. All the people of Judah, and also half the people of Israel, brought the king on his way.

⁴¹ Then all the men of Israel came to the king and said to the king, "Why have our brothers the men of Judah stolen you away and brought the king and his household over the Jordan, and all David's men with him?" ⁴² All the men of Judah answered the men of Israel, "Because the king is our close relative. Why then are you angry over this matter? Have we eaten at all at the king's expense? Or has he given us any gift?" ⁴³ And the men of Israel answered the men of Judah, "We have ten shares in the king, and in David also we have more than you. Why then did you despise us? Were we not the first to speak of bringing back our king?" But the words of the men of Judah were fiercer than the words of the men of Israel.

The Rebellion of Sheba

20 Now there happened to be there a worthless man, whose name was Sheba, the son of Bichri, a Benjaminite. And he blew the trumpet and said,

> "We have no portion in David,
>   and we have no inheritance in the son of Jesse;
>   every man to his tents, O Israel!"

² So all the men of Israel withdrew from David and followed Sheba the son of Bichri. But the men of Judah followed their king steadfastly from the Jordan to Jerusalem.

³ And David came to his house at Jerusalem. And the king took the ten concubines whom he had left to care for the house and put them in a house under guard and provided for them, but did not go in to them. So they were shut up until the day of their death, living as if in widowhood.

⁴ Then the king said to Amasa, "Call the men of Judah together to me within three days, and be here yourself." ⁵ So Amasa went to summon Judah, but he delayed beyond the set time that had been appointed him. ⁶ And David said to Abishai, "Now Sheba the son of Bichri will do us more harm than Absalom. Take your lord's servants and pursue him, lest he get himself to fortified cities and escape from us." ⁷ And there went out after him Joab's men and the Cherethites and the Pelethites, and all the mighty men. They went out from Jerusalem to pursue Sheba the son of Bichri. ⁸ When they were at the great stone that is in Gibeon, Amasa came to meet them. Now Joab was wearing a soldier's garment, and over it was a belt with a sword in its sheath fastened on his thigh, and as he went forward it fell out. ⁹ And Joab said to Amasa, "Is it well with you, my brother?" And Joab took Amasa by the beard with his right hand to kiss him. ¹⁰ But Amasa did not observe the sword that was in Joab's hand. So Joab struck him with it in the stomach and spilled his entrails to the ground without striking a second blow, and he died.

Then Joab and Abishai his brother pursued Sheba the son of Bichri. ¹¹ And one of Joab's young men took his stand by Amasa and said, "Whoever favors Joab, and whoever is for David, let him follow Joab." ¹² And Amasa lay wallowing in his blood in the highway. And anyone who came by, seeing him, stopped. And when the man saw that all the people stopped, he carried Amasa out of the highway into the field and threw a garment over him. ¹³ When he was taken out of the highway, all the people went on after Joab to pursue Sheba the son of Bichri.

¹⁴ And Sheba passed through all the tribes of Israel to Abel of Beth-maacah, and all the Bichrites assembled and

followed him in. ¹⁵ And all the men who were with Joab came and besieged him in Abel of Beth-maacah. They cast up a mound against the city, and it stood against the rampart, and they were battering the wall to throw it down. ¹⁶ Then a wise woman called from the city, "Listen! Listen! Tell Joab, 'Come here, that I may speak to you.'" ¹⁷ And he came near her, and the woman said, "Are you Joab?" He answered, "I am." Then she said to him, "Listen to the words of your servant." And he answered, "I am listening." ¹⁸ Then she said, "They used to say in former times, 'Let them but ask counsel at Abel,' and so they settled a matter. ¹⁹ I am one of those who are peaceable and faithful in Israel. You seek to destroy a city that is a mother in Israel. Why will you swallow up the heritage of the LORD?" ²⁰ Joab answered, "Far be it from me, far be it, that I should swallow up or destroy! ²¹ That is not true. But a man of the hill country of Ephraim, called Sheba the son of Bichri, has lifted up his hand against King David. Give up him alone, and I will withdraw from the city." And the woman said to Joab, "Behold, his head shall be thrown to you over the wall." ²² Then the woman went to all the people in her wisdom. And they cut off the head of Sheba the son of Bichri and threw it out to Joab. So he blew the trumpet, and they dispersed from the city, every man to his home. And Joab returned to Jerusalem to the king.

²³ Now Joab was in command of all the army of Israel; and Benaiah the son of Jehoiada was in command of the Cherethites and the Pelethites; ²⁴ and Adoram was in charge of the forced labor; and Jehoshaphat the son of Ahilud was the recorder; ²⁵ and Sheva was secretary; and Zadok and Abiathar were priests; ²⁶ and Ira the Jairite was also David's priest.

David Avenges the Gibeonites

21 Now there was a famine in the days of David for three years, year after year. And David sought the face of the LORD. And the LORD said, "There is bloodguilt on Saul and on his house, because he put the Gibeonites to death." ² So the king called the Gibeonites and spoke to them. Now the Gibeonites were not of the people of Israel but of the remnant of the Amorites. Although the people of Israel had sworn to spare them, Saul had sought to strike them down in his zeal for the people of Israel and Judah. ³ And David said to the Gibeonites, "What shall I do for you? And how shall I make atonement, that you may bless the heritage of the LORD?" ⁴ The Gibeonites said to him, "It is not a matter of silver or gold between us and Saul or his house; neither is it for us to put any man to death in Israel." And he said, "What do you say that I shall do for you?" ⁵ They said to the king, "The man who consumed us and planned to destroy us, so that we should have no place in all the territory of Israel, ⁶ let seven of his sons be given to us, so that we may hang them before the LORD at Gibeah of Saul, the chosen of the LORD." And the king said, "I will give them."

⁷ But the king spared Mephibosheth, the son of Saul's son Jonathan, because of the oath of the LORD that was between them, between David and Jonathan the son of Saul. ⁸ The king took the two sons of Rizpah the daughter of Aiah, whom she bore to Saul, Armoni and Mephibosheth; and the five sons of Merab the daughter of Saul, whom she bore to Adriel the son of Barzillai the Meholathite; ⁹ and he gave them into the hands of the Gibeonites, and they hanged them on the mountain before the LORD, and the seven of them perished together.

They were put to death in the first days of harvest, at the beginning of barley harvest.

[10] Then Rizpah the daughter of Aiah took sackcloth and spread it for herself on the rock, from the beginning of harvest until rain fell upon them from the heavens. And she did not allow the birds of the air to come upon them by day, or the beasts of the field by night. [11] When David was told what Rizpah the daughter of Aiah, the concubine of Saul, had done, [12] David went and took the bones of Saul and the bones of his son Jonathan from the men of Jabesh-gilead, who had stolen them from the public square of Beth-shan, where the Philistines had hanged them, on the day the Philistines killed Saul on Gilboa. [13] And he brought up from there the bones of Saul and the bones of his son Jonathan; and they gathered the bones of those who were hanged. [14] And they buried the bones of Saul and his son Jonathan in the land of Benjamin in Zela, in the tomb of Kish his father. And they did all that the king commanded. And after that God responded to the plea for the land.

War with the Philistines

[15] There was war again between the Philistines and Israel, and David went down together with his servants, and they fought against the Philistines. And David grew weary. [16] And Ishbi-benob, one of the descendants of the giants, whose spear weighed three hundred shekels of bronze, and who was armed with a new sword, thought to kill David. [17] But Abishai the son of Zeruiah came to his aid and attacked the Philistine and killed him. Then David's men swore to him, "You shall no longer go out with us to battle, lest you quench the lamp of Israel."

¹⁸After this there was again war with the Philistines at Gob. Then Sibbecai the Hushathite struck down Saph, who was one of the descendants of the giants. ¹⁹And there was again war with the Philistines at Gob, and Elhanan the son of Jaare-oregim, the Bethlehemite, struck down Goliath the Gittite, the shaft of whose spear was like a weaver's beam. ²⁰And there was again war at Gath, where there was a man of great stature, who had six fingers on each hand, and six toes on each foot, twenty-four in number, and he also was descended from the giants. ²¹And when he taunted Israel, Jonathan the son of Shimei, David's brother, struck him down. ²²These four were descended from the giants in Gath, and they fell by the hand of David and by the hand of his servants.

David's Song of Deliverance

22 And David spoke to the LORD the words of this song on the day when the LORD delivered him from the hand of all his enemies, and from the hand of Saul. ²He said,

> "The LORD is my rock and my fortress and my
>   deliverer,
> ³   my God, my rock, in whom I take refuge,
>   my shield, and the horn of my salvation,
>   my stronghold and my refuge,
>   my savior; you save me from violence.
> ⁴   I call upon the LORD, who is worthy to be praised,
>   and I am saved from my enemies.
>
> ⁵   "For the waves of death encompassed me,
>   the torrents of destruction assailed me;

6 the cords of Sheol entangled me;
   the snares of death confronted me.

7 "In my distress I called upon the Lord;
   to my God I called.
  From his temple he heard my voice,
   and my cry came to his ears.

8 "Then the earth reeled and rocked;
   the foundations of the heavens trembled
   and quaked, because he was angry.
9 Smoke went up from his nostrils,
   and devouring fire from his mouth;
   glowing coals flamed forth from him.
10 He bowed the heavens and came down;
   thick darkness was under his feet.
11 He rode on a cherub and flew;
   he was seen on the wings of the wind.
12 He made darkness around him his canopy,
   thick clouds, a gathering of water.
13 Out of the brightness before him
   coals of fire flamed forth.
14 The Lord thundered from heaven,
   and the Most High uttered his voice.
15 And he sent out arrows and scattered them;
   lightning, and routed them.
16 Then the channels of the sea were seen;
   the foundations of the world were laid bare,
  at the rebuke of the Lord,
   at the blast of the breath of his nostrils.

17 "He sent from on high, he took me;
    he drew me out of many waters.
18 He rescued me from my strong enemy,
    from those who hated me,
    for they were too mighty for me.
19 They confronted me in the day of my calamity,
    but the LORD was my support.
20 He brought me out into a broad place;
    he rescued me, because he delighted in me.

21 "The LORD dealt with me according to my
        righteousness;
    according to the cleanness of my hands he
        rewarded me.
22 For I have kept the ways of the LORD
    and have not wickedly departed from my God.
23 For all his rules were before me,
    and from his statutes I did not turn aside.
24 I was blameless before him,
    and I kept myself from guilt.
25 And the LORD has rewarded me according to my
        righteousness,
    according to my cleanness in his sight.

26 "With the merciful you show yourself merciful;
    with the blameless man you show yourself
        blameless;
27 with the purified you deal purely,
    and with the crooked you make yourself seem
        tortuous.

28 　You save a humble people,
　　　　but your eyes are on the haughty to bring them
　　　　　down.
29 　For you are my lamp, O LORD,
　　　　and my God lightens my darkness.
30 　For by you I can run against a troop,
　　　　and by my God I can leap over a wall.
31 　This God—his way is perfect;
　　　　the word of the LORD proves true;
　　　　he is a shield for all those who take refuge
　　　　　in him.

32 　"For who is God, but the LORD?
　　　　And who is a rock, except our God?
33 　This God is my strong refuge
　　　　and has made my way blameless.
34 　He made my feet like the feet of a deer
　　　　and set me secure on the heights.
35 　He trains my hands for war,
　　　　so that my arms can bend a bow of bronze.
36 　You have given me the shield of your salvation,
　　　　and your gentleness made me great.
37 　You gave a wide place for my steps under me,
　　　　and my feet did not slip;
38 　I pursued my enemies and destroyed them,
　　　　and did not turn back until they were
　　　　　consumed.
39 　I consumed them; I thrust them through, so that
　　　　　they did not rise;
　　　　they fell under my feet.

40   For you equipped me with strength for the battle;
           you made those who rise against me sink
                under me.
41   You made my enemies turn their backs to me,
           those who hated me, and I destroyed them.
42   They looked, but there was none to save;
           they cried to the LORD, but he did not answer
                them.
43   I beat them fine as the dust of the earth;
           I crushed them and stamped them down like the
                mire of the streets.

44   "You delivered me from strife with my people;
           you kept me as the head of the nations;
           people whom I had not known served me.
45   Foreigners came cringing to me;
           as soon as they heard of me, they obeyed me.
46   Foreigners lost heart
           and came trembling out of their fortresses.

47   "The LORD lives, and blessed be my rock,
           and exalted be my God, the rock of my salvation,
48   the God who gave me vengeance
           and brought down peoples under me,
49   who brought me out from my enemies;
           you exalted me above those who rose against me;
           you delivered me from men of violence.

50   "For this I will praise you, O LORD, among the nations,
           and sing praises to your name.

51   Great salvation he brings to his king,
            and shows steadfast love to his anointed,
            to David and his offspring forever."

The Last Words of David

23 Now these are the last words of David:

        The oracle of David, the son of Jesse,
            the oracle of the man who was raised on high,
        the anointed of the God of Jacob,
            the sweet psalmist of Israel:

2   "The Spirit of the LORD speaks by me;
            his word is on my tongue.
3   The God of Israel has spoken;
            the Rock of Israel has said to me:
        When one rules justly over men,
            ruling in the fear of God,
4   he dawns on them like the morning light,
            like the sun shining forth on a cloudless morning,
            like rain that makes grass to sprout from the earth.

5   "For does not my house stand so with God?
            For he has made with me an everlasting covenant,
            ordered in all things and secure.
        For will he not cause to prosper
            all my help and my desire?
6   But worthless men are all like thorns that are
                        thrown away,
            for they cannot be taken with the hand;

⁷   but the man who touches them
     arms himself with iron and the shaft of a spear,
     and they are utterly consumed with fire."

David's Mighty Men

⁸ These are the names of the mighty men whom David had: Josheb-basshebeth a Tahchemonite; he was chief of the three. He wielded his spear against eight hundred whom he killed at one time.

⁹ And next to him among the three mighty men was Eleazar the son of Dodo, son of Ahohi. He was with David when they defied the Philistines who were gathered there for battle, and the men of Israel withdrew. ¹⁰ He rose and struck down the Philistines until his hand was weary, and his hand clung to the sword. And the LORD brought about a great victory that day, and the men returned after him only to strip the slain.

¹¹ And next to him was Shammah, the son of Agee the Hararite. The Philistines gathered together at Lehi, where there was a plot of ground full of lentils, and the men fled from the Philistines. ¹² But he took his stand in the midst of the plot and defended it and struck down the Philistines, and the LORD worked a great victory.

¹³ And three of the thirty chief men went down and came about harvest time to David at the cave of Adullam, when a band of Philistines was encamped in the Valley of Rephaim. ¹⁴ David was then in the stronghold, and the garrison of the Philistines was then at Bethlehem. ¹⁵ And David said longingly, "Oh, that someone would give me water to drink from the well of Bethlehem that is by the gate!" ¹⁶ Then the three mighty men broke through the camp of the Philistines and drew water out

of the well of Bethlehem that was by the gate and carried and brought it to David. But he would not drink of it. He poured it out to the Lord ¹⁷ and said, "Far be it from me, O Lord, that I should do this. Shall I drink the blood of the men who went at the risk of their lives?" Therefore he would not drink it. These things the three mighty men did.

¹⁸ Now Abishai, the brother of Joab, the son of Zeruiah, was chief of the thirty. And he wielded his spear against three hundred men and killed them and won a name beside the three. ¹⁹ He was the most renowned of the thirty and became their commander, but he did not attain to the three.

²⁰ And Benaiah the son of Jehoiada was a valiant man of Kabzeel, a doer of great deeds. He struck down two ariels of Moab. He also went down and struck down a lion in a pit on a day when snow had fallen. ²¹ And he struck down an Egyptian, a handsome man. The Egyptian had a spear in his hand, but Benaiah went down to him with a staff and snatched the spear out of the Egyptian's hand and killed him with his own spear. ²² These things did Benaiah the son of Jehoiada, and won a name beside the three mighty men. ²³ He was renowned among the thirty, but he did not attain to the three. And David set him over his bodyguard.

²⁴ Asahel the brother of Joab was one of the thirty; Elhanan the son of Dodo of Bethlehem, ²⁵ Shammah of Harod, Elika of Harod, ²⁶ Helez the Paltite, Ira the son of Ikkesh of Tekoa, ²⁷ Abiezer of Anathoth, Mebunnai the Hushathite, ²⁸ Zalmon the Ahohite, Maharai of Netophah, ²⁹ Heleb the son of Baanah of Netophah, Ittai the son of Ribai of Gibeah of the people of Benjamin, ³⁰ Benaiah of Pirathon, Hiddai of the brooks of Gaash, ³¹ Abi-albon the Arbathite, Azmaveth of Bahurim, ³² Eliahba

the Shaalbonite, the sons of Jashen, Jonathan, ³³ Shammah the Hararite, Ahiam the son of Sharar the Hararite, ³⁴ Eliphelet the son of Ahasbai of Maacah, Eliam the son of Ahithophel the Gilonite, ³⁵ Hezro of Carmel, Paarai the Arbite, ³⁶ Igal the son of Nathan of Zobah, Bani the Gadite, ³⁷ Zelek the Ammonite, Naharai of Beeroth, the armor-bearer of Joab the son of Zeruiah, ³⁸ Ira the Ithrite, Gareb the Ithrite, ³⁹ Uriah the Hittite: thirty-seven in all.

David's Census

24 Again the anger of the LORD was kindled against Israel, and he incited David against them, saying, "Go, number Israel and Judah." ² So the king said to Joab, the commander of the army, who was with him, "Go through all the tribes of Israel, from Dan to Beersheba, and number the people, that I may know the number of the people." ³ But Joab said to the king, "May the LORD your God add to the people a hundred times as many as they are, while the eyes of my lord the king still see it, but why does my lord the king delight in this thing?" ⁴ But the king's word prevailed against Joab and the commanders of the army. So Joab and the commanders of the army went out from the presence of the king to number the people of Israel. ⁵ They crossed the Jordan and began from Aroer, and from the city that is in the middle of the valley, toward Gad and on to Jazer. ⁶ Then they came to Gilead, and to Kadesh in the land of the Hittites; and they came to Dan, and from Dan they went around to Sidon, ⁷ and came to the fortress of Tyre and to all the cities of the Hivites and Canaanites; and they went out to the Negeb of Judah at Beersheba. ⁸ So when they had gone through all the land, they came to Jerusalem at

the end of nine months and twenty days. [9] And Joab gave the sum of the numbering of the people to the king: in Israel there were 800,000 valiant men who drew the sword, and the men of Judah were 500,000.

The LORD's Judgment of David's Sin

[10] But David's heart struck him after he had numbered the people. And David said to the LORD, "I have sinned greatly in what I have done. But now, O LORD, please take away the iniquity of your servant, for I have done very foolishly." [11] And when David arose in the morning, the word of the LORD came to the prophet Gad, David's seer, saying, [12] "Go and say to David, 'Thus says the LORD, Three things I offer you. Choose one of them, that I may do it to you.'" [13] So Gad came to David and told him, and said to him, "Shall three years of famine come to you in your land? Or will you flee three months before your foes while they pursue you? Or shall there be three days' pestilence in your land? Now consider, and decide what answer I shall return to him who sent me." [14] Then David said to Gad, "I am in great distress. Let us fall into the hand of the LORD, for his mercy is great; but let me not fall into the hand of man."

[15] So the LORD sent a pestilence on Israel from the morning until the appointed time. And there died of the people from Dan to Beersheba 70,000 men. [16] And when the angel stretched out his hand toward Jerusalem to destroy it, the LORD relented from the calamity and said to the angel who was working destruction among the people, "It is enough; now stay your hand." And the angel of the LORD was by the threshing floor of Araunah the Jebusite. [17] Then David spoke to the LORD when he saw the angel who was striking the people, and said, "Behold,

I have sinned, and I have done wickedly. But these sheep, what have they done? Please let your hand be against me and against my father's house."

David Builds an Altar

¹⁸ And Gad came that day to David and said to him, "Go up, raise an altar to the LORD on the threshing floor of Araunah the Jebusite." ¹⁹ So David went up at Gad's word, as the LORD commanded. ²⁰ And when Araunah looked down, he saw the king and his servants coming on toward him. And Araunah went out and paid homage to the king with his face to the ground. ²¹ And Araunah said, "Why has my lord the king come to his servant?" David said, "To buy the threshing floor from you, in order to build an altar to the LORD, that the plague may be averted from the people." ²² Then Araunah said to David, "Let my lord the king take and offer up what seems good to him. Here are the oxen for the burnt offering and the threshing sledges and the yokes of the oxen for the wood. ²³ All this, O king, Araunah gives to the king." And Araunah said to the king, "May the LORD your God accept you." ²⁴ But the king said to Araunah, "No, but I will buy it from you for a price. I will not offer burnt offerings to the LORD my God that cost me nothing." So David bought the threshing floor and the oxen for fifty shekels of silver. ²⁵ And David built there an altar to the LORD and offered burnt offerings and peace offerings. So the LORD responded to the plea for the land, and the plague was averted from Israel.